Libertarian-Socialism:
American Style

A. ROSE TRIGUEIRO

Copyright © 2019 A. Rose Trigueiro.

All rights reserved. No part of this book may be reproduced, stored, or transmitted by any means—whether auditory, graphic, mechanical, or electronic—without written permission of the author, except in the case of brief excerpts used in critical articles and reviews. Unauthorized reproduction of any part of this work is illegal and is punishable by law.

This book is a work of non-fiction. Unless otherwise noted, the author and the publisher make no explicit guarantees as to the accuracy of the information contained in this book and in some cases, names of people and places have been altered to protect their privacy.

ISBN: 978-1-4834-9647-4 (sc)
ISBN: 978-1-4834-9640-5 (e)

Library of Congress Control Number: 2019900391

Because of the dynamic nature of the Internet, any web addresses or links contained in this book may have changed since publication and may no longer be valid. The views expressed in this work are solely those of the author and do not necessarily reflect the views of the publisher, and the publisher hereby disclaims any responsibility for them.

Rev. date: 3/28/2019

Contents

Introduction 1
Libertarianism 7
    Honoring the Bill of Rights 11
    The Frozen House of Representatives. 25
    America's Lost Check in Her Balance 32
    Ending Prohibition 40
Socialism 47
    Social Security 50
    Healthcare Reform 55
    Getting Control of America's Finances. 65
    Achieving an Auditable Election System 72
Libertarian-Socialism 83
    Reforming Our Broken Judiciary Branch 85
    National Service and the Student Loan Crisis 90
    Only the People Can Protect Privacy 97
    How Americans Came to Distrust Science 107
    Climate Change Is Real, but So Are the Politics ... 112
    Modular Transportation Infrastructure for the Future ... 118
    Fission or Frickin' Fracking. 122
    Radioactive Waste Conundrum 127
    Water for Drinking, Irrigation and Terraforming ... 131
    Social Support with a New Currency 135
Obstacles to Success 143
    The Unsustainable Cost of Continuous Global Conflict ... 144
    America's Dangerous World War II Mythology 151
    Unwinding Jobs Tied To the Defense Department. 161
    Identity in America 166

Introduction

Libertarian-Socialism is a mindset, not about a particular dogma that must be served. It is a way to think about America's issues beyond the partisan paradigm that has this nation trapped on the swinging conservative/liberal pendulum. I was stuck on the Democrat-Republican divide. I had been trying to write things and couch them in a way that I thought people would believe was an objective analysis, but it seemed impossible because there was always a Democrat or a Republican in my head agreeing or objecting vehemently.

I could not finish this book until a couple of other muses entered my head. What if a patriotic American, who is a libertarian, and a patriotic American, who is a socialist, were brought together? Recognizing that their country is in trouble and moved by their patriotism, what would they talk about? Yes, one is a socialist and one is libertarian, but as patriots, they search for a compromise answer. Their Americanism keeps them together in their desire for the real answer. What I am calling Libertarian-Socialism is the common ground these two "muses" helped me uncover and document here.

I bounced between the Democratic and Republican ideologies in my youth until I settled on being a Libertarian. I was a card-carrying Libertarian party member for twenty years before I rejected it as a stand-alone ideology that could be effective. I kept on seeing the ideology being used by the rich to break down the social safety net. Libertarianism has been used to shred the implied contract between the people and the government artfully advocated by the Roosevelts, first by Teddy the Republican and then by Franklin the Democrat.

Libertarian-Socialism is about freeing one's decision-making process from the partisan war. It is a framework for arriving at first what is the problem and then what are the possible solutions. These are outputs as the patriotic libertarian and the patriotic socialist engage in their hypothetical debate. Each is driven by their ideologies, yes, but they are also guided by their patriotism.

Partisanship makes America's problems seem insoluble. Libertarian-Socialism can be a rose-colored prism through which to view American political future. Imagining this dynamic conversation helped me over obstacles to write this book.

Yes, one is a socialist and one a libertarian, but as patriots, they search for a compromise answer. This book represents the pragmatic solution that their mutual Americanism yielded. Their patriotism helped put together an agenda that could be supported by the vast majority of the public.

Admittedly, I was warned by some that I would face opposition from intellectuals claiming that libertarian-socialism was nothing more than historical anarchic-communism. Libertarianism is not anarchy. Anarchy is anarchy and socialism is not communism, it is socialism. I can accept that perhaps anarchic-communism is a thing. The thing that preceded the birth of the Soviet Union and the People's Republic of China, where anarchy led to communism.

However, I am not talking about anarchic-communism, which is not libertarian-socialism. I am talking about Libertarian-Socialism… American Style. Something new, hybrid and not bound by existing political dogma helping to free one's decision-making process from today's partisan war. Libertarian-Socialism is a framework to arrive first, at what the problems are and then engage in a hypothetical debate between the two patriots, the libertarian and the socialist. This process helps one to seek out possible, practical, non-antagonistic solutions. (Note: I either capitalize both libertarian and socialism, mostly at the beginning of a sentence or I do not capitalize either as a visual cue to balance the two isms).

Today's two-party system has become so hostile and polarizing that America's problems seem insoluble. Libertarian-Socialism is a looking glass that erases the alleged differences between us. It can show us what we truly are: a nation of individuals who need to—and want to—be a cohesive, tolerant citizenry. A citizenry without racial, economic, social, or political divisions in their hearts.

Many tell me I am a dreamer. Libertarian-Socialism is just another, feel-good, but impractical worldview. Many would say the same about pedaling to work on a bicycle, too. Many useful benefits at casual glance, but not very practical. However, I do commute on my bicycle. I have been doing it for most of my adult life in the land of cars, Southern California. There is a lot of time to think out there pedaling in traffic. The framework of libertarian-socialism grew in clarity during the commutes.

For thirty years in traffic, I have been riding the bike to a job. There are one hundred thousand pedaling miles on this body. Out there on the bike, I saw further confirmation of the essential truth of the libertarian-socialist point of view. The bicycle helped crystallize that truth for me.

One reason why I ride my bike to work is that I feel free out there on my human powered vehicle. I can cut across a parking lot, ride on the sidewalk, jump a berm or otherwise make my own route on a bicycle. I bend, maybe even break some traffic rules to get where I want to go when I want to get there. The libertarianism of the bicycle is undeniable.

The police mostly ignore my lack of "conformity". When they do not, I have had more than half of my bicycle tickets dismissed in court. It is very libertarian commuting on my bike in traffic. One hundred thousand miles while pedaling for thirty years in traffic in the Land of Cars is quite a lot of miles. The aforementioned patriots in my head concurred that I may be a magnificent bicycle rider.

However, in that same hypothetical conversation, the patriots also concluded that it does not matter how magnificent of a bicycle rider I am. I must depend on other drivers to not make a mistake and run me over, which is a key reason I have survived this long. Additionally and perhaps more importantly, I need these drivers to be competent. Drivers need to be able to adjust and avoid me when I make a mistake.

How is that possible? All these thousands of drivers, driving inches away from me, but I ride on. They have not run me over. They have not killed me while I pursue my libertarian quest for freedom.

They have not run me over these different people: a 90-year-old man, a 50-year-old grandmother and numerous 17 year-old teenagers are among the many souls that drove by me over these thirty plus years. They did not run me over and put their tread on my back.

In this state and in this nation, we have a system where we license people to drive vehicles. It seems to work pretty well. This socialist program of training and licensing individuals before allowing them to operate a motor vehicle helps me in my pursuit of my libertarian goals to be free. And, there it is: my first example of libertarian-socialism manifested in the real world.

During much of the time I have been bicycle commuting, I have used a flag on my bike to increase visibility. I used the Gadsden Battle flag for many years, because it was yellow it made me a little more visible in traffic. Moreover, the "Don't Tread on Me" phrase was/is a cycling pun. That is how this version of the Gadsden Battle flag became the cover of this book.

The patriots in my head have kept up their discussions as I ride my bicycle through traffic. Libertarian-Socialism is everywhere compelling me to complete this book. The most successful aspects of America were created and executed with a libertarian-socialist vision though unnamed as such.

Libertarian-Socialism represents the possibility of a bright future for America. Libertarian-Socialism is the light to show the way, but that light needs to be powered by enlightened debate. Civil discussion between patriots on how to go forward is the fuel for political reform in the United States. Libertarian-Socialism is a way of thinking about any given issue sans ideology. To make sure one is properly balancing issues always imagine the discussion between the patriotic libertarian and the patriotic socialist.

My own personal political evolution fluctuated from Republican to Democrat, but I finally settled on Libertarian for most of my adult life. Though I was a small 'L' libertarian, I did regularly cast my votes for Libertarian candidates. The events of the twenty-first century pushed me toward a more socialist point of view however, which got me shouted out of libertarian meet-ups too. Nonetheless, my previous political leanings are a large part of this hybrid vision. Hence, this book mirrors my own internal political evolution that led me toward libertarian-socialism. First, libertarianism, then socialism, followed by the hybrid political vision that is libertarian-socialism.

As has had been said many times, no army, NO power can withstand an idea whose time has come. I believe the time has come for libertarian-socialism. This is a road map for the nation. It defines an adaptable path to that shining city on the hill that still can be America's ultimate destination. Come, the yellow brick road calls! We can get there!

Libertarianism

Each of the respective isms has its point of view. Libertarians have been often criticized that their point of view lacks practicality. This is especially so when respecting individual rights clashes with supporting the police, convicting beyond a reasonable doubt or even moral rectitude. On 9/11, the truth of the libertarian vision was shown to be valid. The practicality of that political point of view demonstrated itself in the real world.

Fear and suspicion of terrorism has transformed America since, but on that date, Americans acted bravely as individuals. Citizens of the United States launched the only successful defense against terrorism on that fateful day. No plane was stopped by the police. No plane was stopped by the military. No plane was stopped by the government. Despite enormous technological and financial support, the protective infrastructure that Americans paid to be put in place failed completely and utterly.

Today that same technological and financial support for a security-industrial complex is involved in the curtailment of individual freedom and liberty in the name of safety. Despite Ben Franklin's grim statement of reality "Those who would give up essential liberty to purchase a little temporary safety deserve neither liberty nor safety" this nation has done just that; given up essential liberties seeking safety. Americans are afraid and believe that the sacrifice of some liberty and freedom will make them safer. They are wrong. The curtailment of individual liberty and freedom can only make Americans less safe.

On September 11, 2001, the government's inherent inability to protect Americans from terrorist attack was clearly demonstrated. Despite this failure by authorities, free people acting on Flight 93 stopped a plane that was going to hit George W. Bush's office. Thus, the essential core truth of libertarianism was validated in this act of heroism by private citizens. The people protect the president; the president does not protect the people. The power of this nation resides in its free people, which is the core truth of libertarianism and a clear lesson from 9/11.

This seems counter-intuitive, but it is true. The events of September 11 clearly illustrate this self-reliant truth about individual liberty. The cold, harsh reality of that truth is scary and makes Americans want to hand off their safety to big government. Unfortunately, big government cannot handle the responsibility—not in its current incarnation, and certainly not without instituting laws and procedures that would seem totalitarian even to post-9/11 eyes.

When Americans give up their ability to protect their personal freedom, it makes them unsafe. On 9/11, there was a massive failure of the multi-trillion dollar military umbrella over this country. One plane getting loose and being used as a weapon might be understandable. Yet after the first plane had hit, Americans saw no scrambling of fighter jets. In 2016, a CIA blimp got loose and Americans saw F-16s on that UFO in minutes, if not seconds! North American Aerospace Defense Command (NORAD) cost trillions of taxpayer dollars to implement and annually billions to maintain. To see it fail as it did on 9/11 was like watching the coach of one's favorite football team go into the fourth quarter with a 99-0 lead and then lose the game.

It is frustrating that so much money was spent in vain to create safety and then protect that safety if it were threatened. However, what is even more frustrating, to use the football coach analogy again, is that the coach is not fired. Instead, the contract is renewed. Then – to increase the cognitive dissonance – the final bit of insanity comes when the renewed contract comes with a raise! This is essentially what happened to the "coaches" after the massive failure of September 11. In just one example of this, George Tenet, then the head of the CIA, was given a medal by George W. Bush.

Ben Franklin is prophetic. He predicts 9/11 insofar as he sees that to the give up one's rights to be safe is a fool's bargain. It does not work that way. One's safety and one's freedom start on one's own doorstep – always. Franklin thought Americans should never forget this central truth, that their liberty was theirs only if they guarded it actively.

Big government not only failed to uncover the 9/11 plot, it failed to stop any of the four airplanes hijacked on that day. It is the nature of the bloated bureaucratic beast that is government to react slowly. Government is too big and pondering to react to the increasingly fluid and flexible attacks of twenty-first century terrorist organizations.

Only the people can compete with those terrorist organizations. In the years since 9/11, Americans have given away more and more of their ability to defend themselves against terrorists. Every time Americans cede an individual right or liberty, Americans make themselves less safe, not more.

Today, the people aboard Flight 93 would not be able to stop the terrorists. Today, all communications are subject to snooping due to the Patriot Act. Some Department of Homeland Security employee would now cut off the cell phone calls that allowed those people aboard Flight 93 to come to an enlightened decision about what action to take. Perhaps the passengers on Flight 93 fashioned weapons from pocketknives and nail clippers, which would now be denied them. Americans have willingly given up the very things that allowed them to stop the one plane that did not hit its target.

Ben Franklin's words hang in the air at every American airport security line! Perhaps his ghost has been whispering in American ears, because they have begun to embrace a kind of libertarian belligerence. A case can be made that libertarianism is a jungle political mentality of survival of the fittest. Americans have become more accepting of the most aggressive aspects of libertarianism that in the past were rejected out of hand. Americans are also embracing ruthless aspects of libertarianism that push a selfish agenda allowing the rich to create a duplicate private infrastructure inside the public one.

However, despite these abuses there is some truth to libertarianism. The most radical and difficult to accept aspect of true unadulterated libertarianism is elevating the individual to equality with the state and sometimes above the state. The acceptance of that kind of individualism would require a lot more tolerance than Americans are demonstrating right now. Nonetheless, libertarianism has enjoyed a resurgence of late in America, which points to a growing acceptance in the mainstream. That is where this book will start: libertarianism, followed by socialism and then the hybrid vision that is libertarian-socialism.

The following political philosophy is heavily rooted in common sense. There are political reasons, not practical ones, for why much of this has not been implemented. This is the purpose of partisan gridlock. It is used to block legislation that is not sponsored by moneyed power. Libertarianism advocates respecting the liberty of the individual. Only with liberty can change in the name of the people happen. Without power to the people, libertarian-socialism cannot move forward.

Let us explore the libertarian aspects of libertarian-socialism.

Honoring the Bill of Rights

America finds itself on the road toward an authoritarian capitalism that minimizes individual liberty. Libertarian-Socialism seeks to promote the freedom that was the original vision of America's founding fathers. In the beginning of the republic, there was a clear belief in liberty as the guiding ideology. The founding fathers provided a framework from which to progress, adapt, and evolve over the years that is not burdened by divisive, preconceived notions of ideology. In America's genesis, the guiding vision was that the individual's freedom comes before the needs of the state, most of the time. The focus truly was on the individual and their liberty and not what was best for the state or business.

No doubt, things have changed a lot since the eighteenth century. However, they have not changed as much as the politicians and ideologues would have Americans believe. The portrayal of the Bill of Rights as a slaveholder's document misses the point. There is no doubt that there are slaveholder signatories to the Constitution and Bill of Rights. The important thing to remember for today's American citizen is that the Bill of Rights represents a shield for each citizen against the state.

The Bill of Rights is an expert construct to protect the individual against the coercion of the state. The document represents an expert construct insofar as the slaveholder signatories understood what it meant not to be free, as they were experts at relieving others of their freedom and meant to avoid it themselves. However, the expertly crafted protections now apply to all American citizens, not just white male landowners.

This is the great experiment that the United States represents today, freedom for ALL citizens. That is why things are such a mess. Experiments are always breaking new ground. Freedom is messy. People are free to hate each other. Of course, this can lead to the current state of affairs, but freedom allows all outcomes.

The Constitution and the Bill of Rights are still the best weapons against tyranny. Like the wielding of any weapon though, it requires courage. It requires the courage to embrace and exercise the rights that individuals are guaranteed by the Constitution. Unfortunately, individuals have been tempted to turn over too many of their freedoms to authorities seduced by the siren song of safety. The Bill of Rights empowers the individual citizen to create change, but citizens must act and be engaged for positive change to occur. Freedom and individual rights are the real defense against those who would loot the nation's treasury and drive the nation into a ditch.

The first ten amendments to the Constitution have been watered down significantly in today's America. The United States is struggling and must return to its roots to save the republic. Freedom is messy, but it also brings vitality and security in ways that often are not immediately clear. Libertarian-Socialists understand that the individual constitutional rights of the citizens are the foundation of the United States. Upon this foundation, the entire republic rests.

Americans now know that wire-tapping was expanded by the Bush administration almost immediately upon taking power in January 2001. Most Americans also understand that this was an expansion of what the Clinton administration had already put into place. However, most Americans do not accept that these new extra-constitutional powers failed, because to accept it is to accept some scary truths. The wire-tapping failed utterly to provide sufficient warning for the same administration to detect and prevent the terrorism of September 11, 2001. This failure clearly demonstrated the ineffectiveness of dragnet surveillance in the Age of Terror, but somehow most Americans missed this point.

Libertarian-Socialists recognize that 9/11 is the "Day the World Changed"; and not just because the anti-constitutionalists named it that within hours of the attacks. The rampant fear following the September 11 attacks was leveraged immediately to justify all manner of authoritarian actions by the state. September 11th is the day that the Bill of Rights was repealed at airports and other public areas.

Unfortunately, as the founding fathers clearly understood, those in power will use extra-constitutional power to preserve their power, and not to protect free citizens. They will eventually leverage extra-constitutional powers for their own ends, leaving the citizenry out in the cold.

Power corrupts and without the proper checks and balances, the government can do as it pleases and often does without consequence. The rule of law is on life support in the United States of America. There is a remedy and here it is the most progressive and radical of all American documents, the Bill of Rights broken down for the twenty-first century citizen.

> **First Amendment** – Establishment Clause, Free Exercise Clause; freedom of speech, of the press, and of assembly; right to petition. *Congress shall make no law respecting an establishment of religion, or prohibiting the free exercise thereof; or abridging the freedom of speech, or of the press; or the right of the people peaceably to assemble, and to petition the Government for a redress of grievances.*

There has been a chilling effect on this amendment, and it is hard to know where to start. The Supreme Court rulings giving more and more person rights to corporations has been one of the reasons for this chilling effect. As corporations have gained personal rights, corporations have been able to suppress speech by using their deep pockets to sue individuals for speaking out. Additionally, freedom of the press has all but disappeared with the aggregation of media in every form by large corporations. No journalists dare push back against their corporate sponsors.

Large corporations are not truly interested in protecting citizen rights, muckraking, or other such altruistic motives. Rather corporations are motivated by preserving and increasing profit margins. The objective reporting of events does not factor into that equation.

Once it was impossible to own most media outlets in one media market, let alone the entire country. Corporate-written legislation has erased these restrictions. A few large corporate entities control the national media.

Television journalism has degraded seriously over the years to become more of an entertainment outlet than a source of information. Infotainment is what it has become with a minimization of the "info" piece. Just as surveillance increased at the end of the last century, the rules limiting media ownership were relaxed. In 1996, and again in 2003, the relaxation of regulations limiting concentrations of media ownership led to waves of consolidation. This consolidation has made investigative reporting subject to corporate power. Without any significant regulation limiting consolidation, even the corporate rivalries that might fund some investigative journalism are non-existent.

Freedom of the press is not a bad thing; it is a necessity for a functioning republic. The press has a monitoring role to play in the republic. Many conservatives have claimed an out of control "free press" wrongly brought down a presidency in the Watergate scandal. While liberals cheer it as the proper role of journalism in a modern democracy, there is a more complicated story for the libertarian-socialist. Bob Woodward's revelation that Deep Throat was the Deputy Director of the FBI at the time throws the liberal analysis into question. Combining this fact with the fact that Woodward is an ex-C.I.A. agent and more doubt is cast upon the liberal narrative of Watergate.

The legacy of Watergate seems to indicate the possibility of media manipulations facilitated by government officials in partnership with corporate entities. The run up to the invasion of Iraq in search of WMD followed this model. The First Amendment no longer seems to be embraced by the government, but it is a keystone in the republic. First Amendment abridgments are useful in the preservation of power, but it is bad for the individual.

> **Second Amendment** – Right to keep and bear arms. *A well-regulated Militia, being necessary to*

the security of a Free State, the right of the people to keep and bear Arms, shall not be infringed.

The Second Amendment seems rather straightforward. People have the right to keep and bear arms for their personal protection as well as for the maintenance of an independent militia not tied to the federal government. Power to the people must also mean the power to own a weapon. Free citizens must be allowed to protect themselves and not simply depend on the government to do so.

This does not mean that libertarian-socialists believe there should be no licensing or background checks. Individuals are not allowed to drive cars in this country without some modicum of training. Guns are just as dangerous as cars and some type of licensing should be instituted as a matter of public safety. Additionally, felons and the mentally unstable should be prevented from obtaining weapons. To accomplish these goals, a minimal background check and a waiting period does not seem to be a violation of this amendment.

Without a doubt, libertarian-socialists understand that this amendment is the one that has survived largely unabridged into the twenty-first century due to its sponsorship by moneyed power. The National Rifle Association is one of the most effective lobbyists in Washington. The Second Amendment has benefited from this sponsorship from an entire economic sector.

> **Third Amendment** – Protection from quartering of troops. *No Soldier shall, in time of peace, be quartered in any house, without the consent of the Owner, nor in time of war, but in a manner to be prescribed by law.*

Of the ten amendments first added to the Constitution, this is the one that may seem the most archaic. This amendment was a direct result of the British government-quartering soldiers within the homes of colonists before and during the Revolutionary War. This may seem to be a very different world than today, but it is not as different as it seems. In the twenty-first century, there have been several lawsuits in California about police stakeouts using private homes. When these stakeouts extend over many hours or days, there is real hardship to the citizen residents.

Citizens are beginning to question the uncontrolled ability of police to declare private property their own. The federal government continues to use military hardware and tactics in civilian police forces. Police forces across the nation are utilizing military equipment and tactics against the citizenry.

In addition, in direct violation of the Posse Comitatus Act, military personnel are operating on domestic soil without martial law being declared. The Congress and Supreme Court have been terribly silent on these deployments. As obsolete as this amendment seems, events of late have made the third amendment seem less archaic and more necessary than ever.

> **Fourth Amendment** – Protection from unreasonable search and seizure. *The right of the people to be secure in their persons, houses, papers, and effects, against unreasonable searches and seizures, shall not be violated, and no Warrants shall issue, but upon probable cause, supported by Oath or affirmation, and particularly describing the place to be searched, and the persons or things to be seized.*

The Fourth Amendment has been largely repealed through fear. Libertarian-Socialism interprets the amendment's reference to "effects" as including "digital effects" making email as sacrosanct as physical mail. Surprisingly, judges and courts have still not pinned this down as they should have by now.

Most citizens have been convinced that the government has the right to protect Americans from themselves. Things like drug testing, sobriety checkpoints, confiscation of property without due process and dragnet surveillance of all digital actions are settled law according to some. Libertarian-Socialists understand law is never settled and pushing back against unconstitutional law is always required.

The security theater that has been instituted in American airports is in direct violation of the Fourth Amendment as well. Courts have blessed these rollbacks of individual rights at airports as necessary for public safety. There has been no proof that this constitutional violation has made anyone safer.

It was not 9/11 that put the Fourth Amendment under assault, but rather the sobriety checkpoints backed by Mothers Against Drunk Driving (MADD) which broke this ground in the eighties. Libertarian-Socialism accepts that perhaps there are public safety issues that allow the sobriety checkpoints, but there can be too much of a good thing.

A wide variety of checkpoints have been created since and now include: seat belt checkpoints, registration checkpoints, and baby car seat checkpoints. Of course, if any illegal activity is turned up in these unconstitutional stops, courts have allowed it to be used against the individual. The courts used to rule evidence obtained in this manner as the "fruit of a poisoned tree" and disallow its usage. The current incarnation of Prohibition has warped everything.

The War on Drugs justified many constitutional abuses. Once these abridgments to the Fourth Amendment were forced through, they were broadened over time. Now in the name of the War on Terror, the Fourth Amendment seems to be just a memory. Without a Fourth Amendment, the central government has quite a bit more power than the founding fathers intended.

> **Fifth Amendment** – Due process, double jeopardy, self-incrimination, eminent domain. *No person shall be held to answer for any capital, or otherwise infamous crime, unless on a presentment or indictment of a Grand Jury, except in cases arising in the land or naval forces, or in the Militia, when in actual service in time of War or public danger; nor shall any person be subject for the same offence to be twice put in jeopardy of life or limb; nor shall be compelled in any criminal case to be a witness against himself, nor be deprived of life, liberty, or property, without due process of law; nor shall private property be taken for public use, without just compensation.*

Like the Fourth Amendment, the Fifth Amendment has been largely repealed as well. Asset forfeiture laws in this nation have become absurdly confiscatory, since they were first used to prosecute drug dealers in the eighties. Constitutionally it seems clear; assets cannot be seized without due process according to this amendment. Nonetheless, the government regularly does so in a whole host of situations.

The original basis for such asset forfeiture laws is shaky. It was to prevent drug dealers from paying for too much defense in the courtroom, which is questionable on its face. After all, the rule of law requires citizens to have the resources to defend themselves and that they are innocent until proven guilty. Today asset forfeiture represents a significant revenue stream into law enforcement coffers across the nation.

Yes, criminals may have ill-gotten gains to pay for lawyers, but this is a free society. Criminals are not criminals until proven guilty in court. Due process means the state must have evidence of crimes, except in the most extraordinary circumstances. It is with that evidence that the state should obtain a conviction before stripping the citizen of assets. Without the requirement of due process to seize property, asset forfeitures that fund law enforcement entities are unconstitutional.

Shockingly, these forfeitures of assets according to the Supreme Court are somehow exempt from the Fourth and Fifth Amendments. Procedures have been put in place to get assets back, but they force citizens to spend more money. Law enforcement personnel determine at the moment of arrest whether assets are to be seized. Suing police departments to retrieve one's property is not what the founding fathers meant by due process.

Many governments, even America's friendliest neighbor, Canada, now advise their citizens not to carry cash in the United States. This advice is not based on the lawlessness of American streets and fear of bold criminals. Rather the advice is based on the documented actions of police in the United States. Repeatedly, people have cash confiscated from them with the excuse that the person must be involved in criminal activity to be in possession of a large amount of cash.

Nothing seems more totalitarian or more Un-American than making the possession of the nation's currency a suspicious activity.

Depriving individuals of their hard-earned cash based on the whims of police officers is a direct violation of this amendment by any reasonable measure. Not only that, it turns America's police into highwaymen relieving innocent travelers of their valuables.

> **Sixth Amendment** – Trial by jury and rights of the accused; Confrontation Clause, speedy trial, public trial, right to counsel. *In all criminal prosecutions, the accused shall enjoy the right to a speedy and public trial, by an impartial jury of the State and district where in the crime shall have been committed, which district shall have been previously ascertained by law, and to be informed of the nature and cause of the accusation; to be confronted with the witnesses against him; to have compulsory process for obtaining witnesses in his favor, and to have the Assistance of Counsel for his defense.*

As was earlier noted, to have one's assets seized would seriously hinder one's ability to secure Assistance of Counsel. Having a jury pool that is so scarce also makes it difficult for the accused to be tried by peers. Only people with sufficient assets to be able to afford to sit in judgment are available in most jury pools. The growing income gaps in the United States makes a jury of peers a fantasy for anyone in the lower economic classes.

The Sixth Amendment is technically still being honored, though in a practical sense it is in a state of repeal. With the amendment in such a weakened condition, it emboldens the government to introduce things like secret evidence and use testimony of paid informants to convict individuals.

The government now has the power to convict and imprison a citizen based upon secret evidence. One can also be convicted of violating a secret law in this new America. Almost all the law surrounding airport security and the TSA is classified. The ultimate power for the totalitarian state is a book of secret laws that allows government to threaten citizens with secret evidence. There can be no defense in such a trial.

Several lines of argument today assert the president somehow has the power to label an American citizen as an enemy combatant, and therefore, that person loses all Constitutional protections. Citizens need to wake up to the incredible danger of such power; it gives the president the powers of a dictator or a king. Beware of offending a person with such power, because one can become a non-person, non-citizen and prisoner with a word.

The idea that the United States government can indefinitely detain citizens or non-citizens without charge, without trial, and torture them is distressing. With non-citizens, a case has been made that the Constitution does not apply. Libertarian-Socialism believes there are consequences to allowing the American government to treat non-citizens poorly. The Bill of Rights creates a place where human dignity is respected through due process of law, regardless of citizenship.

> **Seventh Amendment** – Civil trial by jury. *In suits at common law, where the value in controversy shall exceed twenty dollars, the right of trial by jury shall be preserved, and no fact tried by a jury, shall be otherwise re-examined in any court of the United States, than according to the rules of the common law.*

The rules of common law, so often denigrated today, actually represent the basis of everything in America's contemporary justice system. The United States is a common law country. In all states, except Louisiana (which is based on the French civil code), the common law of England was adopted as the general law of the state, *except* when a statute provides otherwise.

Common law has no statutory basis; judges establish common law through written opinions that are binding on future decisions of lower courts in the same jurisdiction. Broad areas of the law, most notably relating to property, contracts, and torts are traditionally part of the common law. These areas of the law are mostly within the jurisdiction of the states, and thus, state courts are the primary source of common law. Common law is used to fill in gaps. For example, if a man and woman co-habitate for seven years, the common law suggests they are legally married even without ceremony or license.

The twenty-dollar threshold seems rather low, but the right to civil courts facilitates the rule of law. It would have been nice had this amendment been written in such a way as to index the dollar amount threshold in some way. Interestingly, the founding fathers in another, yet unapproved, amendment do index the rate of expansion for one of their yardsticks. This yardstick exists in the only remaining article of the original Bill of Rights that has not become law. More about that later.

Federal common law is primarily limited to federal issues that have not been addressed by a statute. Libertarian-Socialism believes this amendment is meant to support the idea of jury nullification, but that is for another chapter to detail. Unfortunately, such voting of conscience is now frowned upon in America.

> **Eighth Amendment** – Prohibition of excessive bail and cruel and unusual punishment. *Excessive bail shall not be required, nor excessive fines imposed, nor cruel and unusual punishments inflicted.*

The current state of our prison system now constitutes cruel and unusual punishment. Prison overcrowding is a serious issue nationwide. These issues are real and not to be diminished. To force individuals into cramped quarters where they are often subjected to all manner of sexual abuse is clearly cruel and unusual.

Yet, America's fearful society continues to pass laws and resist reform to reduce prison overcrowding. The United States imprisons a greater number and percentage of its population than any Western nation. Imagine the potential of so many of these people thrown on the scrap heap by America's overzealous law-and-order mentality.

The outsourcing of the costs of imprisoning citizens by contracting to private corporate prisons has created a large lobbying group that ignores the Eighth Amendment. Prison lobbyists only care about making sure the prison cells are filled, because each prisoner represents profit. In a democracy, each prisoner represents a failure of the society. The society should always shoulder the burden of imprisoning citizens. Imprisoning citizens for profit motives skews the outcomes. It also keeps America's private corporate prisons full and profitable.

> **Ninth Amendment** – Protection of rights not specifically enumerated in the Bill of Rights. *The enumeration in the Constitution, of certain rights, shall not be construed to deny or disparage others retained by the people.*

America's "make a new law" society has largely sprung up to curtail the broader rights of individuals that should be protected here. Each time the politicians enact a new law; the power to decide is put into a judge's hands instead of an individual citizen. Libertarian-Socialism urges Americans to step back from this mindset and reevaluate whether it is wise to give so much power to the police, especially as those confrontations become ever more deadly.

With so many laws criminalizing victim-less actions Americans no longer are allowing themselves their liberty. Americans have lost the tolerance required to allow individuals to decide their own affairs. Libertarian-Socialism will always return to tolerance as a guiding precept and requirement for the success of the United States.

> **Tenth Amendment** – Powers of states and people. *The powers not delegated to the United States by the Constitution, nor prohibited by it to the states, are reserved to the states respectively, or to the people.*

This amendment clearly means to preserve the rights of individuals, but fearful Americans cannot seem to embrace these ideals. Americans spend far too much time making laws to abridge individual's rights, and therefore, Americans constrain free citizens from their constitutionally protected right to life, liberty, and the pursuit of happiness. A bright future is there to be had by an enthusiastic embrace of this amendment and the other nine for that matter. That can only happen if America does not let fear get in the way.

There it is, an overview of the Bill of Rights for the aspiring libertarian-socialist. One could be excused for asking the question, is the Bill of Rights still in effect? To the libertarian-socialist, the answer is no.

Consider this: To stop the sale of previously legal alcohol in America, an Eighteenth Amendment to the Constitution was enacted in 1920. This started Prohibition. Years later, in 1933 the Twenty-First Amendment was necessary to repeal Prohibition.

Strangely, though, shortly after this repeal, a new Prohibition was restarted without any bothersome constitutional amendments. The banning of the legal sale and use of marijuana did not require an amendment to the Constitution. It simply required politicians to use the legislature to pass laws, which the Supreme Court then upheld.

This was done just a few years after alcohol prohibition had been repealed. Why did the Supreme Court not declare these laws unconstitutional? What changed in the short time after the Twenty-First Amendment? Libertarian-Socialism aims to bring back the Bill of Rights as the yardstick for freedom.

But wait! There were actually twelve original articles in the first draft of the Bill of Rights, and only articles three through twelve were ratified, though they now represent amendments one through ten in the American constitution. What were articles one and two of the original Bill of Rights? Interestingly, the second of the original amendments was passed much later.

Here is Article II from original Bill of Rights:

> **Article II** – On Congressional pay. *No law varying the compensation for the services of the Senators and Representatives shall take effect, until an election of Representatives shall have intervened.*

This provided protection against congressional pay hikes, preventing a sitting Congress from giving itself a raise. Any increase in pay would not go into effect until the following House election. This proposal was resurrected 203 years later when it became the Twenty-Seventh Amendment to the Constitution in 1992!

Again, the founding fathers predicted conflicts and provided a statutory basis to address the situation—such foresight! That means that eleven of those original twelve have now been passed, but what about the last remaining one?

> **Article I** – Providing for a truly representative republican democracy. *After the first enumeration required by the first article of the Constitution, there shall be one representative for every thirty thousand, until the number shall amount to one hundred, after which the proportion shall be so regulated by Congress, that there shall be not less than one hundred representatives, nor less than one representative for every forty thousand persons, until the number of representatives shall amount to two hundred; after which the proportion shall be so regulated by Congress, that there shall be not less than two hundred representatives, nor more than one representative for every fifty thousand persons.*

The explosive growth of America's population outstripped these visionary representation numbers. This was followed on by the abolition of slavery and women's suffrage, which changed the demographic electoral equations dramatically. Nonetheless, the founding fathers expected the House of Representatives to continue to grow with the growth of the electorate. For over one hundred years the central government followed this formula, but then they stopped. Inexplicably, for a century the House of Representatives has been stuck at a little more than 400 individuals!

The Frozen House of Representatives

The House of Representatives was meant to be the People's House. Despite popular belief, America is not a democracy, but rather a representative republic. That means that the representatives, who are democratically elected over set periods, do the business of government as representative proxies.

At the beginning of the republic, to get each of the states to sign on to the new Constitution, each was given two votes in the Senate no matter the size of their populations, thereby making sure that each state was equal in that representative body. However, for America to be a true representative republic there had to be a legislative body that was based upon population. That body became the House of Representatives.

The framers of the Constitution and the Bill of Rights intended that the total population of Congressional districts should never exceed 50,000 to 60,000. This fact cannot even be debated as the text of the original article demonstrates that some threshold was on the mind of the Constitutional Convention, even if that threshold was never agreed on. Currently, the average population size of the districts is approaching 700,000! That is a more than ten-fold deviation from a standard that was nearly cemented into the constitutional framework of the nation at its founding.

Clearly, the founding fathers recognized this ratio as vital to a functioning representative republic. George Washington agreed that the original representation proposed in the Constitutional Convention (one representative for every 40,000) was inadequate and supported an alteration to reduce that number to 30,000. This was the only time that Washington expressed an opinion on any of the actual issues debated during the convention.

In Federalist Paper No. 55, James Madison addressed the claims that a 50,000 to 1 representation ratio was insufficient by writing that the major inadequacies would be cured over time by virtue of decennial reapportionment based upon the census. Madison acknowledged that there were some inadequacies at the House level in the original Constitution, but that every ten years the census would allow for adjustments. Madison expected these inadequacies eventually to go away, not to be set in stone by the central government.

Adding to this degradation of representation, in the early twentieth century the United States government abandoned the principle of proportionally equitable representation. Prior to the twentieth century, the number of representatives increased every decade as more states joined the union and the population increased.

In 1911, Public Law 62-5 raised the membership of the House of Representatives to 433 with a provision to add one permanent seat each upon the admissions of Arizona and New Mexico as states. As provided, membership increased to 435 in 1912. However, in 1921, Congress failed to reapportion the House membership as required by the United States Constitution after the decennial census. Then, in 1929, Congress passed the Reapportionment Act of 1929, which capped the size of the House at 435. The count has been stuck at this 435 number ever since.

Freezing the count has led to inadequate representation. This inadequate representation has only become more inadequate as time as gone on. Two states have been added, since the Reapportionment Act of 1929 and yet the count has stayed at 435! This arbitrary ceiling not only ignored new states, but also ignores that the nation's population has increased rapidly. Despite the population increase, the membership of the House of Representatives has stayed static for a century. If Washington, DC no longer seems to represent the will of the people. It is because it does not.

The population increase that has occurred since the early twentieth century warrants change in the size of the House, but it is not the only reason nor does it represent the biggest jump in voters. The actual number of eligible voters doubled immediately with women receiving the vote in 1920. This is about the same time that the number of representatives was frozen at 435. Certainly, this freezing seems to be a purposeful attempt to dilute representation. After all, doubling the number of voters should justify doubling the number of representatives to something approaching one thousand seats. If not that number, then a lesser increase would still be warranted.

The current size of 435 seats means one member represents on average about 650,000 people; but exact representation per member varies by state. Four states – Wyoming, Vermont, Alaska, and North Dakota – have populations smaller than the average for a single district. This one situation, that these low population states get better per capita representation in the House of Representatives than high population states, should be enough to call for a revamp of the size of the House of Representatives. The Senate's two seat per state configuration serves the small states, but the House is where the populous states are supposed to have more representation, not less.

Many would argue that the current size of the House is one of practicality. They would argue that increasing the number of members would create chaos and nothing would ever be done in Congress. Libertarian-Socialism would argue that there is not much positive and useful being done right now, so how can the status quo be advocated?

The reforms libertarian-socialism advocates in American society and in the political system might seem quite dramatic. However, these reforms are based on the original precepts of the nation. It is quite illustrative of how far America has strayed from the original ideas of the founders. Arguing for a return to these principles sounds so revolutionary to many citizens, when they first hear of this proposed amendment to the Constitution, but it is a founding ideal.

Clearly, America should increase the size of the House; there is no question about that. It is only a matter of by how much to increase it. The objection that more than 435 would be impossible to manage is no longer tenable in the twenty-first century. Technology has advanced to the point that video conferencing is a viable option. Additionally, the amount of Congressional staff each representative has is a clue to what the true size of the House of Representatives should be. If these non-elected staffers were limited, it would free up quite a bit of space for real representatives of the people as well as the money to pay them.

Other democracies seem to get by with more than 435 members without chaos ensuing. The House of Commons in Britain, which was one of the first people's bodies in the Western world, has more than six hundred members. Another great western democracy, Germany, has more than six hundred members in its Bundestag. These parliamentary bodies serve populations that are one-fifth the size of the American population. If Americans had similar representation, there would be three thousand members in the House. Without question, the United States has fallen behind the curve of representative democracy.

Libertarian-Socialism advocates an initial doubling of the size of the House of Representatives. This would be achieved by bisecting all current districts. Libertarian-Socialism further advocates increasing the House membership by 50 percent in five-year intervals leading to next census. This would still leave the United States far short of the original vision of its founders. A case could be made for continuing to increase the size until a one to fifty thousand ratio is achieved. Of course, by finally ratifying the last of the original articles that made up the Bill of Rights, this would be constitutionally mandated to happen.

Forcing a smaller ratio of people-to-representative will lead to more than two thousand House members. That is a big number, but the United States would thus begin to immunize the House of Representatives from the corruptions of money. With so many votes to swing a majority, it would become ever more impractical to influence the House via lobbyist money.

There would also be an increase in the number of voices that could be heard on the national stage. America has stagnated. The solutions to the nation's problems seem insoluble only because of the narrowness of the vision of those in politics today. This narrow vision is directly related to the freezing of the House that has disenfranchised the individual voter.

An increase in the size of the House of Representatives is also an organic obstacle to gerrymandering. Gerrymandering leads to extreme views at the political representative level. Extreme views are required to win the gerrymandered districts. The smaller districts of an expanded House are harder to gerrymander. The smaller districts make irregular shapes an exception rather than the rule.

Indeed, for there to be an electable third party, or even a fourth party, this House expansion must happen. The House increase would begin the process of giving new political voices an opportunity to be heard. This is why the duopoly of Democrats and Republicans will fight tooth and nail for the status quo.

Additionally, the size of the House of Representatives drives the size of the Electoral College. The Electoral College size is determined by the number of seats in the House of Representatives and the number of seats in the Senate plus three extras for Washington DC. That puts 538 seats in the Electoral College. Consequently, with many more seats in the House of Representatives the nation would have smaller districts in the Electoral College as well. The smaller districts also make it more difficult to "game" elections.

Smaller districts in the Electoral College give the people better representation due to the granularity that is provided. Of course, the smaller districts are not going to necessarily bring about a fix to the popular vote not matching the Electoral College outcome. This popular vote disconnect is an anomaly that happened only once in the nineteenth century. Oddly, the twenty-first century has seen it happen multiple times, in the elections of George W. Bush and Donald Trump.

These divergences of the popular vote from the Electoral College certainly smell like election tampering. Technological changes are facilitating the gaming of the Electoral College. More and smaller districts make this gaming more difficult. Conversely, the elimination of the Electoral College could make it easier to game the presidential election by making it completely unauditable. The smaller districts allow for auditing the presidential election, but more on that later.

In the beginning, it made sense for each elector to go to DC and represent the constituents from the home district. Travel and communication were not what they are today. Sending a responsible individual to report counts from particular districts across the country made sense at the beginning for these reasons. Though those reasons are no longer valid, citizens now have more reasons to doubt their will is making it to Washington. The Electoral College districts represent auditable chunks of the election that the people must not relinquish.

Interestingly, the founding fathers have something to say on this matter of gaming the Electoral College. The founding fathers did not envision political parties and therefore they did not foresee their effect on the Electoral College. The founding fathers did live to see the growth of the political parties, however. In their opinion, the parties were horrific parasites on the political system. In their later years, after the formation of the republic, many founding fathers spoke quite clearly in opposition to changes brought about by political parties.

Political parties were born in the eighteenth century, but really started to take off in the early nineteenth century. Their actions had an effect on the original architecture of the representative republic, specifically the Electoral College. Political parties almost immediately saw the extra power it would give them if an entire state went toward their party versus the opposing party. As a political party gained control of a statehouse, they would institute a winner take all system. This meant any opposing party needed to take the same actions in states where they controlled the statehouse to compete. This is how we arrived at the "winner take all" inequities (*the victor of a majority of Electoral College districts in any given state receives all electoral college votes for that state*). Unsurprisingly, the machinations of the political parties led to this undemocratic process today.

James Madison was always concerned about the people's representation in the central government. He was one of the first to speak out against this "winner take all" practice. Alexander Hamilton also joined him in condemning the winner take all elector system that the statehouses were implementing at the behest of political parties. In fact, the two of them tried to get a constitutional amendment to prevent the states from sending electors to the Electoral College via this methodology. Both men understood this diluted representation and disenfranchised voters.

Here we see again that the architecture that the founding fathers put in place for this representative republic was an incredible balancing act, a balancing act that came under attack from power brokers immediately upon implementation. What was so incredible and unprecedented about this balancing act, was the weighting of the individual so heavily against all power: military, police and government. From the very beginning, the founding fathers gave the individual much weight versus traditional institutions of power.

The bias toward the individual in the affairs of the state and law seems radical to today's eyes. The mere idea that the justice system should free ninety-nine guilty men before imprisoning one innocent is anathema to most Americans today.

If the United States is to continue, a healthy dose of tolerance needs to be injected into the American soul. Americans must allow their neighbor to have the same freedom that they want for themselves as well. That is the only way it works. Everyone gets the freedom or it slowly degrades to a ruling elite and then dictatorship and tyranny.

The process of electing national leaders is awash in money and corrupted by it. Americans know this, and campaign reform is regularly on the national agenda. However, no matter what laws are passed, real reform escapes the nation. Increasing the size of House of Representatives means it will take much more money to control voting majorities in a House with many hundreds of new members. Increasing the size of the House will bring about a kind of campaign reform along with all the other aforementioned benefits of the appropriate per capita representation for the people.

The United States may have to build a new legislative building, but that is no reason to listen to Democrats and Republicans whine about their lost duopoly. Spending money on this new larger House of Representatives is an intelligent use of funds. It is an honest investment in representation. An investment in a game-changing vision to return the United States to the citizens. An investment to help the people take their rightful place in the leadership.

America's Lost Check in Her Balance

Jury nullification is the lost check of the people against government overreach. Americans are taught that the Constitution was meant to create a system of checks and balances that would prevent tyranny. It is a basic premise in American civics that each branch of government acts as a check on the others. If the system seems out of balance today, it is because America has lost an original check in the balancing act. There is a lost check and that is the power of a jury to return a verdict of not guilty based upon their own moral judgments about the law and its application. Jury nullification allows a jury to return a not guilty verdict based upon their conscience thereby blocking the application of a law on a case by case basis.

The founding fathers meant to ensure that the government had to go to twelve citizens every time it intended to relieve another citizen of property or freedom. This has long been a controversial topic in America. It is another radical idea of the founders, because it puts the power to interpret the law into the hands of the twelve average citizens on the jury. These twelve peers are supposed to be able to vote their conscience and decide for themselves whether the law applies or the law is just.

The government has dealt with those who speak of jury nullification by throwing them in jail. This was done in Denver in 2015. Two men were arrested and charged with several felonies for handing out pamphlets about juror rights. There are few more effective ways to suppress an idea than to imprison advocates. The charges were eventually dropped due to the Supreme Court precedent supporting the concept in the case SPARF vs US (1895) as well as free speech justifications.

One of the keystones of a libertarian-socialist agenda must be the citizen empowerment that jury nullification represents. America's future rests upon allowing individual citizens to vote their conscience in the courtroom. It is a vital burden of citizenship as it relates to checks and balances on justice and the power of the central government.

Currently, the levers of government power are in the hands of the wealthy and big business lobbies. The jury room can be a source of change. That is why so much power lines up to try to control jurors. While the power of jury nullification exists, state courts and prosecutors are not required to inform jurors of this power. In addition, judges around the country have routinely forbidden any mention of jury nullification in the courtroom.

The power to the people ethos that jury nullification represents requires an incredible amount of tolerance from each American. Freedom is truly a messy, uncontrollable business. The most basic tenet of freedom is expecting and wanting individual citizens to think for themselves. Politicians fear citizens that think for themselves.

With jury nullification, Americans need to trust another twelve Americans at least as much as they trust the judge or the prosecution. It is easy for moneyed power to separate Americans with divisive noise and fear mongering. On many different issues, this is the game plan to stymie forward progress. Divide interest groups until support evaporates. Americans will need to tolerate many differing opinions, lifestyles, and religious beliefs to forge an alliance large enough to bring jury nullification into the public forum.

Jury nullification opponents will claim anarchy. Cries from the law-and-order crowd of anarchy and chaos always target the citizenry's most fearful visions. With the media saturated in numerous flavors of cop shows coupled with endless news cycles of gruesome crimes drawn from all across the country, it is easy to be fearful. Nonetheless, Americans must trust other Americans. It is the United States, so without unity, there is no country.

Jury nullification is not advocating anarchy, but asking the people to fix what politicians, police and courts have failed to fix.

Libertarian-Socialism does not advocate anarchy, but it does advocate a society that does not imprison such a huge percentage of its citizens. An overwhelming majority of Americans want the bad guys to go to jail and will put them there. However, the current situation has too many decent, though flawed individuals being put into prisons.

The whole idea behind the American jury system was to allow ninety-nine guilty men to go free before imprisoning one innocent man. This system is a political foundation that elevates the individual to the level of the state unless there are compelling reasons to do otherwise. Americans seem to have forgotten how destructive imprisonment is. The founding fathers and the Constitution created a justice system that might free ninety-nine guilty individuals.

Such a system is a huge check on government power. Police can arrest people all day, but if they cannot convict them through constitutional means, their power is checked. The power of the central government to impose its will upon the people is limited. Jury nullification is a first line check on government power.

Jury nullification means the government should not pass laws that do not have wide support within the population. In fact, jury nullification requires more than ninety percent of the people to agree with a given law for it to be effectively enforced. The ninety percent figure is not just hyperbole. It is a number based upon the jury system put into place by the architects of the United States justice system. Though in practice, the government can lower this percentage significantly through venue changes and the very real "chilling effect".

Given the requirement that a jury of twelve must agree unanimously to provide a guilty verdict, divide one by twelve, which allows for an eight percent disagreement percentage. This leads to a minimum ninety-two percent agreement threshold in the populace for successful implementation of a given law. What an ingenious check on a government's power to imprison its own people. With the requirement of ninety-two percent agreement, how could America have become the largest jailer of its own citizens? America has an enormous prison population and imprisons more of its citizenry than any other nation by raw numbers and by per capita measurements. For example, the US imprisons seven hundred people out of one hundred thousand, which is four to five times the rate of other Western nations.

Private prisons exacerbate this problem through their lobbying. For example, corporate prison money supported efforts to stop Colorado's marijuana legalization efforts. Given the large percentage of marijuana offenders in prison, legalization has a direct effect on the bottom line of corporate prisons. The prison lobby uses its money to push for ever more draconian laws requiring imprisonment along with opposing any rollbacks to existing mandatory sentencing laws.

Corporations not being actual citizens or people pursue their balance sheets. That means corporations lobby to imprison more people, since their business is imprisoning people. Americans must monitor bad people for sure, but Americans must also monitor those who judge and imprison other Americans. A failure to do so means Americans are imprisoned in large numbers. Only with a return of a justice system that allows a juror to vote their conscience can the citizenry roll back laws instituted largely to help corporate prisons to be profitable.

The Rodney King beating and the subsequent trial of the officers involved illustrates how out of balance the justice system has become. The King case was a long time ago, but his words still hang in the air. "Why can't we all just get along?" Many Americans were dismayed by the acquittal of those officers. The evidence was right there on videotape of how he was beaten. Sure, Rodney King was not a pillar of virtue, but even if he were on PCP, which is arguable, his treatment by the arresting officers was clearly police brutality. The George Holliday tape showed him on the ground and cuffed with multiple officers continuing to deliver blows to an obviously helpless individual. How can that not be police brutality?

A closer examination of the 1992 trial shows the jury is not to blame here. A broken justice system compelled them to deliver the verdict that those in power desired or be jailed themselves. The Rodney King jury received strict instructions from U.S. District Judge John G. Davies that they could not convict the officers if the Los Angeles Police Department had trained them to beat Rodney King in this manner. Such jury instructions would appear to favor the defense of the officers. Surely, jurors would not believe they could vote their conscience in the face of these instructions.

Perhaps jurors wished to vote their conscience, despite those instructions. Unfortunately, the judge's strict instructions on the criteria for conviction were in direct conflict with the truth of the power embodied in a real citizen jury. Such narrow jury instructions represent unconstitutional powers conferred upon the judge. Contempt of court is a very real threat, and judges have enormous latitude in its application, imprisoning people on the spot if they so choose.

This is why police officers in the twenty-first century continue to be acquitted repeatedly for beating and killing citizens. These unconstitutional jury instruction powers allow judges to define for the jury what criteria they may use to convict and this has warped the system. For example, if a police officer is trained to beat people then they cannot be convicted. This may be a judge's opinion, but a juror can use their own criteria, because the power to decide lies with the jury.

When there is no faith in a system to deliver justice, there is unrest. Following the police officers' acquittal of beating King, there were riots that on the surface had a racial component. However, the riots were more than the black versus white rioting that the media and government portrayed it as. Many groups of people hit the streets to protest the acquittal. Beyond race, there seemed to be a subconscious desire to send a message to the police. That although the police officers owned the courtroom, and were supported by the system, the streets were still owned by the people in those South Central Los Angeles neighborhoods.

The Clinton administration came in and retried the case in 1993 before a grand jury. This was a further demonstration of the broken state of the American justice system by violating constitutional protections against double jeopardy. The central government got around double jeopardy restrictions with the torturous logic of claiming that the officers had violated Rodney King's civil rights. In the end of the retrial, some police officers were convicted, but there were varying degrees of responsibility assigned to them.

Despite the ultimate outcome, the retrial only made the whole situation worse by failing to address the strict instructions given to the original jurors. The waiving of double jeopardy restrictions to avoid addressing the unconstitutional jury instructions that judges have been allowed to force upon helpless jurors amounts to attempting to use two wrongs to make a right. Judges continue to be allowed to threaten jurors with contempt of court unless they interpret the law as the judge instructs.

The path to the unbalanced justice system in America has been driven by fear. The fear of being victims, the unrest and crime of the mid-twentieth century and the growth of the national security state, have all combined to create this imbalance. The national security octopus is an obstacle everywhere when discussing ideas of individual liberty and is often instrumental in setting precedents in the courts. The national security role simply cannot be ignored.

In 1989 when George Bush Sr. went into Panama and dragged Manuel Noriega back to the United States for trial, many questioned the legitimacy of such a military action. America's own international legal experts deemed the military intervention legal, of course, but much of the world was less convinced. This invasion needed a lawful conclusion to be more than simple kidnapping, so Noriega was put on trial for drug trafficking among other crimes.

Unfortunately, for Bush Sr. the American people spoke out in the courtroom. The people questioned the legitimacy of the president's kidnapping of a foreign leader. The reality was that the government could not get a conviction. To the government's dismay, the American jury failed to convict Noriega. Global opinion of the invasion appeared confirmed by the American jury.

The jurors could not agree that Noriega deserved to be imprisoned for the alleged drug trafficking that he was charged with at trial. Some citizens questioned the United States' interpretation of international law that allowed the invasion of Panama. Others questioned the legitimacy of using the military to capture and kidnap a foreign head of state. America's own system of justice could not and would not convict Noriega.

As much of the rest of the world believed this was a violation of international law, it was also a violation of American law, according to America's own citizen jury. The ambivalence of the citizen jury is understandable, because this is congruent with the first leaks of the CIA's operations in Central America. The revelations about the Contras being funded by drug smuggling threw into doubt American accusations of drug trafficking by Noriega.

Many critics of the president's action referenced Noriega's previous high standing with the American government as an ally in the Drug War. Noriega seemed to be receiving punishment for some transgression in his dealings with the CIA. This was the contention of many observers. Media outlets were waiting for Noriega to start singing, so that a more complete picture of what was going on in Central America would be revealed.

The administration could not stand for Noriega to escape conviction. The United States military had been mobilized to invade a sovereign nation, then captured the duly elected leader of that country, and brought him back to the United States. There had been much international protest over this Christmas Eve invasion. To be unable to convict the man in an American court would have been an embarrassment for Bush Sr.

Such an outcome was not truly a possibility, though. Once it became clear the jury would not convict, it was marched before a group of government operatives and presented with "secret evidence". What was the secret evidence that never saw the light of day? We still do not know. National security was invoked to justify secret evidence. We may never know what was said or shown to the jury, but once the government had the meeting with jurors, the desired outcome was delivered.

Perhaps the government officials simply told the jury that they either convict Noriega or go to jail themselves. The details of the secret evidence are classified, so the actual details of the secret evidence remain unknown. Noriega went to jail, but it was far from a legal trial. After all, it was an obvious case of jury tampering. Such tampering is a constitutional offense, but by then, the government had already largely exempted itself from such mundane constraints as the Constitution.

The above legal precedents have led to the power of juries being seriously curtailed. One of the original intents of the jury system is to ensure a constant vote of the people on the laws and the justice system. To accomplish this, America must address the aforementioned constraints on juror consciences, but more than that, Americans must fund jury service. There is no way the average working American can get a jury of his peers. All their peers are average-working Americans too and cannot serve without pay.

Too often all a defendant's true peers are working for companies that do not compensate for jury service. This must change. The federal government, meaning the taxpayers, must fund this essential part of the American justice system for their own protection. With verification by pay stubs and/or tax returns, jury compensation should come somewhere close to an individual's real day to day pay. There has to be a more reasonable recompense for this essential citizen service than what is currently being done.

There will be cries about the expense. Libertarian-Socialists know in their hearts that funding jury service is funding freedom. For the accountants, there is the promise that rolling back the police state could reduce costs related to imprisoning such a large percentage of the populace, but it is hard to know that for sure. Whether jury nullification reduces costs or not, the price for freedom is what it is. Freedom cannot be had on discount.

The people are an unruly mob in the eyes of many in the halls of money and power. The people are also viewed as dangerous by the one percent. Together the people, the poor, the blue collar, the middle-class, all outnumber the moneyed, the powerful, the wealthy titans of business, and that is why those same titans are constantly beating the drums of fear. Jury nullification represents a true threat to the current power structures in the United States.

The moneyed and powerful will invariably go to their default propaganda that the criminals will take over to spark the fear that gives them control. This is the subtle, incessantly whispered incantation of television shows like "CSI this" and "CSI that" or "Law and Order this" and "Law and Order that". It will only be a brave and tolerant citizenry that will be able to resist this drumbeat of fear. Libertarian-Socialists must remind Americans that the criminals have already taken over. The jury box is where justice will be done. Americans can choose to trust each other or continue to keep faith in an obviously broken justice system.

Ending Prohibition

Prohibition nearly destroyed civil society in the United States once, which makes its current incarnation so baffling. Prohibition has been central in the steps that have led to the Constitution and the Bill of Rights being rendered so impotent. This new prohibition has curtailed individual freedom for reasons more political than practical.

The excuse for this strong reversal of individual rights, this War on Drugs, was and is to increase public safety, but public safety has not increased. In fact, in some areas public safety has eroded in ways directly related to prohibition. With prisons overflowing and a continuing drug epidemic, the War on Drugs is clearly a failure. This failure was evident early on by almost any reasonable metric. Nonetheless, the prohibition continued to be fueled by the politics of power and money well after its obvious failure.

The earlier prohibition on alcohol demonstrated the shortcomings of criminalizing the victim-less behaviors of otherwise productive citizens. The policy financed crime. It was destructive to law and order in general. In the final analysis, alcohol prohibition was a miserable failure creating many more negative effects in society than alcohol abuse ever did.

Worth noting here is the fact that the original Prohibition, alcohol prohibition, required an amendment to the Constitution and when Prohibition was finally ended, the Constitution was amended again. For some reason lawmakers decided they no longer had to follow these constitutional protocols in the War on Drugs. No such amendments were required for banning a wild growing plant like marijuana, which had been legal since the beginning of the nation, and even grown by the founding fathers of the United States.

The dangers of rolling back individual rights in the name of this new prohibition are self-evident now. Prohibition has led to corruptions of money and corruptions of motivation at many levels. The United States has little positive to show for the hundreds of billions of dollars that has been spent fighting the War on Drugs.

The costs to personal liberty from the War on Drugs have been staggering. American prisons are overcrowded and overflowing with non-violent drug offenders. The United States has eliminated many constitutional protections in a rabid pursuit of this tragic War on Drugs. However, after generations of this war one is hard-pressed to find successful outcomes justifying the dismantling of individual rights.

Prohibition has failed in its stated goal to reduce the harms of drug abuse. The policy has been very much about preservation of power and money rather than public safety. Marijuana users tended to be liberal voters. It is not hard to imagine conservative strategists recognizing this fact and beginning a gradual whittling away at the liberal voter base.

The Constitution limits the powers of the central government to prevent exactly this type of coercive power, which can be wielded so easily for political gain. This is why constitutional boundaries are so important. Had such coercive power been properly checked, conservatives could not have been lured into violating their own small limited government vision. Prohibition offered too great a weapon against the liberal voter base for conservatives.

In the beginning, intellectually consistent conservative thinkers, like William F. Buckley, Jr. opposed the War on Drugs, but they were ignored. The political motivations were too powerful for conservatives. Many a liberal leaped upon the anti-crime bandwagon too. The anti-crime rhetoric was so effective in getting a politician elected. Liberal politicians trying to burnish their own image have acted to rollback individual rights even more passionately than conservatives have at times.

Certain basic practical realities must be adhered to in a free society. One of those pragmatic realities is that criminalizing victimless behavior destroys freedom. The altering of one's mood chemically is as old as human history. Most of the so-called recreational drugs have a molecular structure similar to naturally occurring substances in the human body. These drugs have a molecular make-up that allows them to bond to specific receptors in the brain, mimicking the effects of chemicals normally manufactured by the body in association with certain emotions. Chemically altering ones mental state is a normal human behavior.

Humans are electrochemical engines. The makers of the many anti-depressants on the market today have proven this fact over and over. For some odd reason, the government has allowed these anti-depressant drugs to be used on the populace, while prohibiting other psychoactive drugs with much longer track records of use, such as marijuana. Anti-depressants are even being given to children, sometimes with suicidal results.

Why do government and medical experts claim to be able to read the minds and emotional states of free individuals and to mandate what molecule bonds in a satisfactory manner to an individual's own brain receptors? This is another government overreach, making laws against mental states turns the state into the "thought police."

The drive to alter mental states is a strong one. With the government cracking down even harder on mainstream recreational drugs, some people have begun to turn to all kinds of alternatives. Marijuana, for example, will show up on drug tests for months while a prescription opioid will only show up for a few days at most. This climate compounds the motivation to use an opioid, as employment can often be contingent on passing a drug test.

This is the true source of the opioid epidemic. The ability to be on the right side of the law and to get a job are very powerful motivators to avoid something like marijuana and use Vicodin instead. For the well off, a prescription painkiller has no "risks" at least as far as law enforcement and employment is concerned. The desire to comply with the law coupled with normal human behavior and addiction lead directly to the opioid epidemic.

There is talk of making opioid abuse a hard felony and imprisoning the abusers instead of rolling back the draconian drug laws. Americans seem to have only one solution; illegality. They can see no other solution than imprisonment. The nation must move beyond this abuse then punishment cycle, even if the corporate prison lobby would prefer the nation continue its punitive ways.

Libertarian-Socialism prefers to take a more practical approach, understanding that not every naturally occurring chemical that could alter a person's mood can, or should be, made illegal. The current American tendency is to regulate and come up with laws making each plant molecule illegal. This process is usually followed by chemists working feverishly to create artificial versions to avoid the law.

The artificial version can then be legally sold until that molecule is then made illegal. Laws against the different plants are terribly impractical, because chemists then set out to copy plant molecules in such a way as to make a synthetic version of some naturally occurring drug to avoid the law.

The government has a horrible record in the drug arena. The old alcohol prohibition or the anti-depressant caused suicides are illustrative of the government's terrible track record, but there are others. The federal government and the FDA actually blocked release of a safer cigarette.

In the eighties, the tobacco industry had developed a safer, smokeless cigarette, a vaping precursor. Essentially, the safer cigarette was a plastic tube that delivered the nicotine without the tar and other carcinogens. The FDA labeled it a drug delivery system and prevented it from coming to market. Of course, it was a drug delivery system, but so is the standard paper cigarette.

Despite much shouting to the contrary, the tobacco industry is not quite as evil as the tax-hungry politicians have made them out to be. The reality is that the government bears a huge responsibility for continuing the lung cancer and emphysema deaths that have occurred over the last thirty plus years. Preventing the tobacco companies from bringing their safer cigarette to market has preserved decades of tax revenue to state, local, and federal government through sin taxes. The government's main mission should be the well-being of its citizenry without significantly curtailing personal freedom, not preserving revenue streams.

Americans know there is a need for relief in the overloaded

justice system. They are finally becoming concerned about the fact that the nation imprisons more of its population per capita than any other nation on Earth. How can America be called the land of the free in light of that statistic? One of the most beneficial consequences of drug legalization would be the family reunions that would happen all across the country as non-violent drug offenders returned home.

The monetary consequences of this war have been enormous. Annually, a trillion dollars of controlled substances may be hitting the streets and that is after America has already spent at least that amount to prevent it. Economists really do not know how much is actually hitting the street, untaxed.

The free market has been speaking loudly on this issue for some time now. Throughout history, America has obeyed the free market most of the time. The free market would willingly pay taxes adding another beneficial consequence of ending prohibition. Another exciting beneficial consequence of legalization is taking the money out of the hands of violent criminals. Serious consideration of legalization sends shivers down the spine of every cartel leader.

If Americans want to reduce prison overcrowding and take the pressure off the police force so it can tackle real crimes against the public order, Americans must begin to relax these draconian drug laws. It should start with the federal prohibition on marijuana. Marijuana is relatively safe as recreational drugs go.

Death from an overdose of marijuana continues to be unproven, while alcohol poisoning is a well-known cause of death in medical literature. In the current climate, investigating the toxic effects of marijuana requires better data than the black market can supply. In this regard and in many others, prohibition makes Americans less safe.

Many question how drug legalization could work, but the marijuana legalization occurring in many states now lays out a road map. This approach causes the least harm to society by limiting prison populations and generating some tax revenue, too. Economically, the benefits of federal marijuana legalization could be dramatic for the American farmer. By allowing farmers to grow these high profit crops, Americans can begin to reduce the subsidies that have become little more than corporate welfare for agribusiness.

More importantly than all of these benefits is the hope that bringing it out of the shadows can help the nation understand and curb its appetites. Americans do not know why the United States leads the world in drug consumption. They are incredulous when faced with the fact that with five percent of the population of the world, Americans consume over fifty percent of the world's cocaine and opioid production.

Libertarian-Socialism seeks to assuage the nation's obvious despair by ending imprisonment for drug abuse. However, libertarian-socialism does not have an answer to why Americans have such a prodigious appetite for drugs. That is for the nation to discover for itself through the transparency made possible by legalization. To find out, the United States needs to look in the mirror.

This problem has become a national security issue. It appears the Chinese may have already zeroed in on this weakness as they flood America with fentanyl. To the Chinese, turnabout is fair play. They once fought the West in the Opium Wars to prevent their own country from being swamped under the importation of opium. Unfortunately, the tables have turned in the 21st century.

Socialism

Libertarianism is easy to trace back to the founding principles of the United States leading some Americans to see it as the patriotic "ism". Socialism on the other hand has not been ardently embraced by a similar number of Americans. There is a common, but erroneous suspicion that it violates the principles of the founders.

In truth, America shares a complex relationship with socialism. The fact that the nation retains Social Security and other social services along with the recent popularity of the Bernie Sanders campaign illustrates that more complex relationship between Americans and socialism. Socialism is not the great evil it has been made out to be by moneyed power. Every society has socialism. Socialism is not really an ideology, but a property of all societies. All societies have some flavor of socialism. They have some collective action that they must do together to survive. The military is the most basic of all socialist enterprises.

For Americans to reject socialism when they are getting "Social" Security checks and Medicare seems foolish to other nations. Socialism clearly has a place at the table in the United States, despite rhetoric claiming socialism to be an unnatural state of affairs and therefore unsustainable. The embrace of libertarianism in the United States has at its core this idea that libertarianism is very basic and natural. This law-of-the-jungle mentality certainly appeals to those arguing that tough choices need to be made as it relates to Social Security, Medicare and other aspects of America's social safety net. Of course, libertarian-socialists recognize that socialism is also basic and natural to humans. In fact, it is so basic and natural to the human condition that socialism may be encoded into human DNA.

Libertarianism is seen as the natural state of human society, while socialism is portrayed as an unnatural state that is not sustainable. However, every society has socialism. Socialism is not an ideology, but a property of cooperation that exists in any organized human community.

Imagine this scenario, humans are on the plains of Africa many millennia ago and different tribes control different waterholes. One tribal leader at one waterhole makes the people of the tribe "pay" in some kind of currency—hunting, or work or whatever the "leader" deems useful—to get a share of water or a share of the hunt. This "strong" leader with some well-chosen allies controls the rest of the tribe. Access to some very basic resources is restricted by the leadership of this hypothetical tribe.

In contrast, at another waterhole and in a different hypothetical tribe the leader operates a different regimen on water access and sharing the spoils of the hunt. In this tribe, basic resources are shared equally among tribal members. For example, access to the water hole is not restricted by tribal leadership. Leadership rewards hard working or especially talented hunters with surplus from the kills, but only after the tribe's basic needs have been met. In this tribe, leadership operates more in partnership with the regular tribal members. This tribe's leadership team has determined that access to basic resources makes everyone stronger. The rising tide raises all the boats is how Franklin Delano Roosevelt use to say it.

Now imagine a lion pride came walking down upon the plain searching for a waterhole. The pride is on the plain occupied by these two hypothetical tribes. The waterhole where the spoils of the hunt were shared more equally—where access to water, for example, is a shared and a protected right by being a part of the tribe—In that tribe, they are all stronger. They all work together. They fight off those lions.

The lions move on to the other waterhole where access to the spoils of the hunt is strictly controlled by leadership. At this waterhole the members, as a cooperative unit, are weaker. They lack cohesion, since they do not share in the spoils of the hunt or have equal access to water. Their desire to work and fight collectively is weakened. Their basic health is weaker as well. Since access to food and water is rewarded regardless of the basic needs of the individual, their collective health must suffer. This tribe loses to the lions. Their selfish DNA is removed from the human gene pool and the lion pride takes over that water hole! The cooperative tribe survives to pass on its DNA.

Socialism is likely a part of human DNA. Socialism, collective action and human success are tied together. Socialism is not pie in the sky dreaming. It has been a real and proven survival mechanism for groups of humans since time immemorial.

Social Security

The balancing of America's budget has been a political hot potato for a long time. Recent changes to the tax code make Social Security a target more than ever before. Make no mistake about it; Social Security is called Social Security, because it is a socialist program. As the architect of the program, FDR would certainly have seen himself as something of a socialist as well. A close look at the twentieth century shows socialism is just as much a part of American success as libertarianism.

Social Security is a socialist program originally championed by a socialist president. However, Social Security as it exists today is not the pay-as-you-go old age pension for retired workers envisioned by Roosevelt. Social Security is no longer FDR's vision, but represents a conservative reworking of a socialist program too popular to legislate away. Anti-socialist crusaders could not kill Social Security outright and instead planted a time bomb to destroy it.

In 1980, Ronald Reagan was elected on promises to cut government overspending. His budget director, David Stockman, was in the spotlight almost immediately. Seemingly, every day, Stockman was under fire for recommending another program be cut. There was much outrage among Americans. To a political animal like Reagan, it was clear that Americans wanted to pay less for government, but they did not necessarily wish to cut any programs. Reagan realized that Americans wanted something for nothing and he dutifully delivered.

Reagan and his brain trust made the politically astute decision to fire David Stockman. The American people only wanted lower taxes, not less government. When Reagan actually tried to do what he said he was going to do most Americans balked at their government program being cut. Much of the limited government rhetoric Reagan had espoused during the campaign ended up unrealized due to political calculus.

Libertarian-Socialists accept that the dead body that lies at America's doorstep in the form of trillions in debt today is the responsibility of the people as much as the responsibility of politicians. A lack of honesty and attention by the citizenry helped create this mountain of debt and that cannot be overemphasized. The libertarian-socialist agenda cannot and will not succeed without an empowered and engaged populace. Engagement means assessing the budget numbers and making hard choices.

The tax cutting folklore that has grown out of the Reagan presidency is illustrative of the lack of attention citizens have paid to the American tax code. The American people chose to look the other way as Reagan's tax cuts caused enormous budget deficits. Americans gladly accepted Reagan's assertion that the nation could get something for nothing.

Again, libertarian-socialism is not here to indict the Reagan presidency, but rather to illustrate to the people how not paying attention and not being honest leads to poor governance. Right in front of the people Reagan hired none other than Alan Greenspan to rework the Social Security program. Reagan and the Congressional Democrats made a deal to "save" Social Security. This huge rework of Social Security is directly responsible for much of today's debt.

Reagan's cutting of the tax rates in the United States has entered into American mythology. To the unobservant, it appeared that Reagan's budget and tax code rework was a tax break. Historically this tax break has been trumpeted as massive. However, when one looks more closely at what the Reagan administration did in the eighties, the tax break is far less impressive.

Normal income tax brackets were standardized and overall income taxes were lower, that is true. Largely unreported was that Social Security taxes were expanded to affect more Americans. This is actually a shifting of tax burdens to the lower income brackets, because Social Security is only applied up to a certain income level.

Most Americans never see their income exceed the amount

that is subject to the tax. The rich and well-off not only enjoyed an income tax cut, but had a large portion of their incomes exempt from Social Security tax. By expanding the number of workers subject to the tax, increasing the retirement age and instituting a tax on Social Security benefits tax revenues increased. However, the revenue increase for the social program's support was shifted to the lower income brackets.

The tax changes specifically brought in more revenues on the backs of workers who have been paying ever since. The revenue increase was not due to the "Laffer Curve" as was claimed at the time. The Laffer Curve stated that cutting taxes increases economic activity. This increases revenues in the form of increased tax receipts due to the increased economic activity. The eighties are often pointed to as proof of this economic principle, but the increase in tax revenue under Reagan was due to a straightforward increase in taxes on closer inspection. None of the Social Security's extra revenue was actually protected from use in the general fund and was summarily spent.

The stealthy shifting of the tax burden into a trust fund to pay for future benefits allowed the government to have a much greater day-to-day cash inflow. The excess tax revenues could now be spent by looting the Social Security Trust Fund and replacing dollars with IOUs. Reagan's alleged tax cuts actually confirmed Keynesian economic ideas.

All throughout the eighties, the government ran huge deficits even with the extra cash the new Social Security revenues brought. There were huge increases in defense department spending with no cuts elsewhere to pay for these increases in revenue outflow. The greater government spending led to an economic boom in the eighties just as the great socialist economist John Maynard Keynes predicts.

An engaged citizen needs to understand what happened to the tax code in the eighties. Social Security had been a "pay as you go" program, but under the Greenspan rework of the tax code, Social Security began collecting more taxes than it needed to meet its obligations. The standard income taxes did go down under Reagan. There is no doubt of this fact. This served as a massive tax cut for the rich, yes. It was a pittance for the middle class and poor due to the large increase in Social Security taxes.

This tax system has clearly benefited the very wealthy far more than it does average Americans. After thirty years, Americans see enormous income and wealth inequality compared to the situation before the Reagan/O'Neill tax deal putting Greenspan's work into law. The 2017 tax reform is even more lopsided in favor of the wealthy.

This is the true legacy of the Reagan/O'Neill tax reform to save Social Security. A disproportionate amount of the tax burden was shifted to the wage earners with the promise that the extra tax dollars being collected would be saved in a Social Security Trust Fund. Americans are just starting to learn about the state of the Social Security Trust Fund. It is not good, since it only holds IOUs.

Libertarian-Socialists recognize that Social Security tax dollars are owed to the working class people. Libertarian-Socialists also recognize that the Speaker of the House during the Reagan years, Tip O'Neill, a Democrat, was instrumental in getting these changes through the Congress. That recognition simply serves as more confirmation of the political duopoly.

America's elected leaders have been removing the money from the Social Security Trust Fund for some time now. That money has been allegedly invested in special government bonds. Nonetheless, the Social Security Trust Fund is actually empty having been spent on the Bush/Cheney upper income tax cuts, Afghanistan, Iraq and numerous military engagements all across the globe. There is now a big fat IOU sitting in that account in the form of government bonds. The most recent tax reform of 2017 puts in doubt whether those IOUs can be redeemed.

The people hold a promissory note for trillions that the American government is beginning to seem a little wobbly about paying back. This is the true reason that Standard and Poor's corporation and the Chinese rating agencies downgraded American debt from AAA to AA+ in 2011. The American government has already begun to default on some of its very real debt obligations in the eyes of those looking from the outside, like the Chinese and Europeans. To objective observers, shifting the goalposts on the Social Security debt by changing the rules is cheating to avoid default. Other holders of American debt are rightly concerned about the earnestness of the American government.

There continues to be a huge revenue stream from Social Security taxes. Bill Clinton's budget surpluses were based upon the enormous surplus that the Social Security system was running at that moment. Now in the twenty-first century, America needs the Clinton surpluses, but there is only debt. Libertarian-Socialists understand the American citizen has paid for a secure retirement. Libertarian-Socialists also understand that it will cost money—trillions, in fact, to pull it off.

Americans want these entitlement programs to go on despite the financial obstacles. Americans need and want a social safety net. Working Americans are owed these dollars. Americans want unemployment and disability insurance, along with Social Security and Medicare. Despite these wants and desires, America's social programs need to be restructured. The libertarian-socialist also understands that built-in cost of living adjustments need to be recalculated if America is to create anything sustainable.

A simple rule change to remove the cap on when income is subject to the Social Security tax would go a long way to balancing revenues with outflows. Currently, the Social Security Tax is only on the first hundred thousand or so of income, anything above that is tax-free as far as Social Security is concerned. Of course, most Americans never see this enormous tax break. If the average American knew they would see no reason that so much income should be exempt, but such a simple rule change is widely opposed by moneyed power.

To salvage Social Security as a pillar of an American social safety net, it needs to return to its original model as a "pay as you go" program. America's greatness is locked up in her people. When promises to the people are broken, especially after years of working, civil unrest can follow. The people are owed Social Security, and the government reneges on this important promise at its own risk.

Healthcare Reform

Ever since the creation of Medicare, government-run healthcare has been demonized to the point of the ridiculous. When Medicare was first proposed in the sixties, it was condemned as socialism that would end the American way of life. Of course, it was socialism. Americans like their socialism as long as it is not called socialism. For generations now the government-run system of Medicare has been relatively successful. Medicare actually represents a reasonable facsimile of a responsibly operated government program.

Medicare is quite expensive though, especially because health care prices have increased far faster than inflation. It would be disingenuous not to admit that less than twenty years after its inception in 1965, the program had to be reconfigured to raise the taxes that paid for it into the twenty-first century. In addition, program costs since the rejiggering in 1982 have increased at a staggering rate. This cost increase has been directly related to ballooning prices of medical procedures in the United States.

Nonetheless, Medicare has been a success, insofar as the recipients are happy. Americans in general continue to support it. Medicare is a costly program, but one gets what one pays for in America. A good program that costs money is expected. The out of control healthcare costs in the United States are less expected.

In the past, Americans have allowed politicians to pass "feel good" legislation without properly accounting for the costs inside and outside government. The 1986 Emergency Medical Treatment and Active Labor Act, which required hospitals to provide stabilizing treatment for patients with emergency medical conditions, including childbirth, without first demanding evidence of ability to pay is a perfect example of "feel good" legislation. Though this is surely the humane course, this unfunded mandate has been putting a social burden on private medical providers for decades. Estimates put that burden at over 1 billion dollars, which is put on the backs of the insurer of the last resort, hospitals.

The law requires these individuals to be treated, but provides no money to pay for it. It is worth noting though that this is proof that Americans do see healthcare as a right. Neither the patriotic socialist nor the patriotic libertarian believe people should be turned away from the emergency room just because they are poor. Logically, that service should not be forced on the hospital without someone paying the cost. Currently, private industry simply passes the costs to the rest of the insured population.

These costs are not small. The costs of noncollectable debts from emergency room treatments cannot be ignored. Without a doubt, this billion dollar pass through is one of the reasons medical costs have skyrocketed. Government has put a burden on private medical care providers and these costs are passed on to the subscribers of the system. These hidden cost burdens are hard to account for as the costs and profit margins are not very transparent.

In 2008, the election of Barack Obama sent the pundits to their chalkboards. Their shared belief was that the people wanted some kind of universal healthcare. Americans knew the Republicans were not going to deliver it, hence the Democratic landslide in 2008. Democrats took this as a mandate for change as well on the health care front. They immediately set to work on healthcare reform.

Unfortunately, what the Democrats produced was incremental at best. Essentially, Obamacare, boiled down to one thing, the insurance companies agreed to stop denying people coverage due to pre-existing conditions and in return the government made it illegal not to own the product. This is the Republican plan of the nineties that was offered up as an alternative to the Clinton administration plan. Obamacare creates a captive clientele for the medical insurance industry, but does nothing about costs.

The alleged reform that is Obamacare is nothing more than the aforementioned trade-off. When the subsidies are thrown in most of America recognizes this as a bad deal, though they also recognize the need that Obamacare met. The situation that preceded Obamacare demanded reform that is undisputed among Americans.

The answer that Americans want and the answer that Americans can afford are at odds is what the alleged experts are saying. That is a false choice. Americans are already affording the most expensive system on the planet. The problem for Americans is that this system works best for the financially advantaged, but let's down most of the rest.

The United States as a country spends more of its GDP on healthcare than any other developed nation. Both the patriotic libertarian and the patriotic socialist understand that Americans cannot get something for nothing, but they also understand America is currently overpaying for inferior service. Despite paying very high premium rates as a country, Americans do not have the longest life spans or lowest infant mortality rates. Frankly, there is very little that Americans can point to as successful in the current health care system, with the exception of high-end specialty and experimental treatments. It is no wonder that Americans have become so skeptical that Washington, DC can produce anything effective.

American skepticism is well founded. At the beginning of this century, the Medicare Part D drug benefit was signed into law by George W. Bush and touted as a huge success. A closer look reveals that the only victory was for drug companies. Within the bill, the government and the people were denied the ability to fight for better prices. The law has specific language preventing the government and the people the option of importing the very same drugs being sold at lower prices in countries all across the world. Why is this? The American people are subsidizing drug prices all across the globe. Bush's alleged reform ended up being an industry-written and industry-favoring legislation. Obamacare substantially continued this model if one is honest.

Medicare Part D was little more than a repackaging and institutionalizing of the Medigap plans that had been in existence for decades. To get on the Medicare drug benefit, the subscriber had to pay about the same price to get about the same benefit that already existed in private industry supplemental insurance. Of course, the drug companies had no problem with this legislation, because it allowed them to lock the government and the people into this two-tiered pricing system, where Americans continue to pay more than the rest of the world. Obviously, real patriots, whether they be libertarian or socialist, do not believe in discriminating against their fellow Americans. This is the real history of what has masqueraded as healthcare reform in this country for too long.

Corporate-written bills are passed through the state legislatures and Congress under the guise of reform and assistance to the people. This is where Obamacare is most vulnerable to criticism. Though the healthcare reform does subsidize the enrollment of many into medical insurance, it does nothing to control prices. This ends up putting huge pressure on businesses, especially small businesses and sole proprietorships to pay for Obamacare-mandated policies, which set premiums, and benefits based on whatever the insurance companies want to charge. Americans know how necessary healthcare reform is, but if Obamacare is the healthcare reform, they also know it is not sustainable. Paying for healthcare remains one of the No. 1 issues facing United States citizens.

Obamacare mandated that everyone had to buy health insurance to spread risk creating a complete pool for American insurers, but it did not provide a public option for this mandate. What a boon to the insurance companies! They now had a captive clientele. To try to make this more palatable to Americans, there are subsidies to help lower income individuals afford the healthcare insurance. These subsidies are just more public money into the coffers of insurance companies. It has the tangential effect of making poor Americans feel like beggars as well.

As terrible as it is, no coverage as an option does sometimes pay-off. Americans that might take the risk of not having insurance, sometimes actually make out better in the end, if they are lucky enough to be healthy over a long period. Obamacare eliminated this terrible gamble as an option with mandated coverage.

Conservative rabble-rousers claim Obamacare has been rejected by a large segment of people, because it was socialism. A closer look uncovers the opposite though. Americans support Obamacare. A segment of the opponents are actually advocating greater socialism, because Obamacare does not go far enough. Subsidizing rates without controlling costs is a foolish bargain, especially without a government-backed option. The threat of a single payer system is what private industry must compete against for it to reform itself.

The lack of a universal single payer system is destructive to the "ownership society" that conservatives often trumpet as the heart of the American dream. The patriotic libertarian has convinced the patriotic socialist that an ownership society does give citizens a greater stake in outcomes and that is not a bad thing. They agree that the ownership society is at the heart of the American dream, but the poor healthcare system in this nation threatens Americans with economic ruin and bankruptcy. The libertarian-socialist recognizes the need for the whole of a society to bear the healthcare burden so that individuals are free to pursue their economic and personal goals without fear of financial destruction through illness.

Anti-socialist rhetoric always avoids talking about the huge amount of public money in the healthcare system already. Medicare, Medicaid and Veterans Administration healthcare dollars cover more than half of the healthcare expenditures in this country. These are left out of the debate, because for the most part they are effective and efficient programs. These examples of a public option dilute the argument that private insurance makes healthcare delivery more efficient than public insurance ever can.

Medicare runs on a low administrative overhead, while the private sector is running at many times that overhead. It is no wonder private industry would not want to compete with the public option. Medicare has proven public funded healthcare can be run efficiently. Somehow, the horribly inefficient government is outperforming the private sector. The private sector claims to be more efficient than government, but Americans are learning that the private sector tends to send its efficiency savings to executive bonuses.

Medicare's efficiencies are tied to fee schedules that regulate costs. The difference between this fee schedule and something known as the UCR, the usual and customary rate, is extraordinary. Insurance companies negotiate with doctors for a rate that is always some percentage of this UCR, never the full amount. Medicare's negotiating power means it has the best cost per procedure among insurance providers.

This is where the public option would give everyone a look at the huge disconnect between the UCR, and Medicare's fee schedule. Clearly, it makes sense for the government to step in and start imposing a fee schedule on everyone. An industry-written bill will never go there and fix the fee schedule gap. The medical insurance monopoly will not voluntarily solve this problem. Industry-written legislation will always extend the medical insurance monopoly rather than breaking it.

Running healthcare to serve a bottom line is a flawed model for private health insurance. As a for-profit enterprise, the system currently sees sick individuals as a hit to the bottom line that must be mitigated. Libertarian-Socialists realize that healthcare should be a public utility that is regulated. When libertarian-socialists look at social problems of this nature, they instinctively understand that the government is the place where such problems can be addressed.

Medicare is not meant to be run as a for-profit exercise or even as a break-even enterprise. A nation's health care costs are whatever those costs are. A single payer system represents a nation's commitment to its citizenry. America should take care of citizen health needs as part of the nation's budget regardless of cost. It must do so as a matter of national security and national ethics. Any freedom is always subject to one's health and enlightened societies understand that without health, citizens have nothing.

There is no question that as the population ages, Medicare only gets more costly. Medicare was created to address the fact that older Americans could not get affordable health coverage in the twentieth century. Older citizens are obviously going to have more health problems than younger individuals do. Therefore, the idea of expanding Medicare to encompass a greater percentage of the population and get some spreading of the risk makes sense in actually lowering per capita costs.

Medicare enjoys the support of Americans. Unfortunately, that program came from a government that no longer exists – a government that is dependent upon re-election by serving its main constituency, the average American. Expansion of Medicare should have been one of the first steps on the road to reforming health insurance in the twenty-first century.

Unfortunately, moneyed interest groups are writing legislation in the United States now, so that means that Medicare expansion has not been given serious attention. Medicare expansion would immediately call into question the private insurers business model. Medicare can never be considered as an option by the corporate authors of legislation. It is a direct threat to the industry's business model.

Right now, the health of the United States is running in the wrong direction and further wrangling in Washington, DC is not likely to help the state of healthcare in America. If America does not expand Medicare to everyone, it is not clear how else to deal with Obamacare's Medicaid subsidy sunset leaving too many people not covered. Medicare expansion is one way to reform Obamacare by moving the subsidized population there. Why continue to send the subsidies to private industry, which has been crying crocodile's tears about their government revenue windfall anyway?

A first step allows America to collect real data on the health of the uninsured population by opening Medicare to them. Who will jump in? How much will it cost? What are the common health issues plaguing Americans? The United States needs to collect this data to reform the system anyway, so why not do it while helping uninsured Americans.

Medicare expansion means America gets to collect real data on the state of the uninsured in the nation. It is unfortunate this will end another revenue stream for private industry. The healthcare industry's various players have had their chances to make it work. They have only their own greed to blame. People are dying because of ridiculous pricing of insulin in the United States. Action must be taken.

This is the first step to real healthcare reform, opening Medicare to the uninsured. The collection of data and the immediate assistance to an ailing citizenry represent immediate dividends to the investment. It is, of course, only a stopgap measure. Nonetheless, it would begin to put into practice some kind of public option to compete against the private sector.

In the final analysis, the cost of medical care must be addressed. The costs of drugs and procedures will need to be regulated in some way. If these costs are regulated, then it will be a boost to the profit margins of insurers, since they are unlikely to lower the premiums as proven by history. Since insurers will not pass on these savings to the private citizen unless there is a public option, it becomes clear a public option is mandatory for a successful reform.

Somehow, the United States found a trillion dollars to bailout financial entities during the Great Recession of 2008-09. This was after the country had already evaporated a trillion dollars in the futile chase for weapons of mass destruction in Iraq. All that money was public taxpayer money that really did not serve domestic taxpayer interests. The interests of the oligarchy are served too often by taxpayer funds, while the needs of domestic citizenry go begging.

Finding the money is an investment in the future. Just as the patriotic libertarian has convinced the patriotic socialist that the ownership society is a positive goal, the patriotic socialist has convinced the patriotic libertarian that a health care safety net is a necessary support to that ownership society. Those who oppose some public healthcare option are unpatriotic.

America can afford some public option, especially in the current private insurance climate. An expansion of the public option will make it clear to private insurance industry executives that they must work to provide affordable insurance. Most likely that fix will mean some kind of regulation of healthcare fees. Private health insurance can work with the public option to create a positive synergy that controls health care costs or private health insurance can continue to be uncooperative and lose their monopoly altogether.

Currently, Americans are paying a high premium for less positive outcomes. A private-public partnership remains an option. The current model in the United States is pretty much a proven failure. Despite industry protestations, developed nations all across the world have some universal healthcare. All have some component that is a public option. These plans also require individuals to get health insurance, but that is in conjunction with a public option or at least heavy regulation of healthcare premiums and provider costs. Universal healthcare systems vary in the extent of government involvement in providing a single payer or public option healthcare delivery system, but there is always some public component, because there simply must be.

The developed nations of the world have created several good examples on how to structure the public component in healthcare. In some countries, such as the Great Britain, Spain, Italy, and the Scandinavian countries, the government has a high degree of involvement in the delivery of healthcare. Access is based on residency, not on the purchase of insurance. Other countries have more eclectic delivery systems based on obligatory health insurance with contributory insurance rates related to salaries or income. Employers and employees also usually fund the plans jointly. Sometimes, the funds are derived from a mixture of insurance premiums and government taxes. Some countries, such as the Netherlands and Switzerland, operate via privately owned, but strongly regulated, private insurers.

Most current universal healthcare systems were implemented in an attempt to adhere to Article 25 of the Universal Declaration of Human Rights of 1948, a declaration from the United Nations General Assembly. This declaration was signed by most of the Western nations and almost every signatory now operates a universal healthcare system. The United States did not ratify the social and economic rights sections, including Article 25's right to health. Americans today are paying the price for not recognizing the real necessity of basic healthcare. Healthcare should truly be a right. It is a life and death issue and one that cannot be left to a for profit delivery system.

All of the aforementioned international universal healthcare systems function relatively well, though not always inexpensively. The measure of their success can be seen in life spans, infant mortality, and many other metrics of the overall health in the population of other developed nations. Very few Americans can sit back and claim that healthcare delivery in this nation is not horribly broken and does not need reform given the real health statistics.

Americans simply must find the money to fund the Medicare expansion. Libertarian-Socialists realize that no amount of classified, black budget security expenditures can protect the nation from the scourge of disease. Health of the citizens is a primary security issue in a very direct way.

There are models all across the planet that the United States can adopt or tweak. Americans need something better than what is being delivered. Making private businesses pay for such a basic social goal, as Obamacare requires, is not correct. It is especially unfair to small business owners and sole proprietors who make up such a large portion of the American business fabric. Conversely, it is no less unfair to kick the uninsured into the street and provide them nothing but catastrophic care.

It is in the best interests of this nation for the uninsured to be covered by Medicare while the nation hashes out a better solution. It is also in the best interests of this nation that this extra burden not be borne by small business, but by the taxpayers as a whole. Any objections related to costs are hollow. If anything has been made clear in the twenty-first century, this nation has had no problem finding money off budget to support military action in the name of national security. The health of this nation has finally risen to that level. Healthcare simply is a right in an enlightened and developed society.

Getting Control of America's Finances

One of the greatest criticisms of socialism is the spendthrift mentality that sometimes infects the politicians, people and administrators of social programs. The lucrative feedback loops of such initiatives are temptations for each of the players in a program whose revenue stream is taxes. Social programs are expensive and must be administrated with an eye on the fiscal limits of an economy. Despite the possibility for corruption, America wants and needs a social safety net. Social Security and healthcare are only a portion of the social programs America's people cry out for, but funding is a challenge.

America still has the money to do the right thing, but no longer enough to do EVERY thing. Looking at American debt problems, one can be excused for believing that cutting spending is the only answer. This enthusiasm for austerity should be kept in context, for it has been used for decades to drive tax cut upon tax cut for upper income tax brackets. It has caused financial uncertainty and the hollowing out of the middle class. These tax cuts have led to oceans of red ink.

Cut, cut, cut the taxes is the mantra, but after decades of tax cuts the expected benefits have not materialized, certainly not for the greatest majority of Americans. For over thirty years, America has fed the upper income brackets all the tax cuts they can handle, either borrowing the money or reducing social programs to pay for it. By now, it is clear this is not effective or responsible revenue policy given the current monetary situation.

In day-to-day expenditures, a huge portion of the budget resides in Social Security, Medicare and military spending. This is well documented and understood. It is much less understood that the over collection of tax revenue that was supposed to be put in a trust to pay for Social Security in the future has been pirated and used to fund tax cuts for higher income brackets. Were the Social Security Trust Fund packed with the cash that has been over collected in the previous decades, the budgetary crisis would not be a crisis.

Neither the patriotic socialist nor the patriotic libertarian can ignore a crumbling infrastructure, failing schools, armies of homeless, and the growing list of problems caused by neglect in this nation. A course change is in order. Investment in roads, healthcare, education, telecommunications and technology are necessary.

There are a host of other infrastructure-related capital expenses that can yield dividends. The exact dividends are impossible to calculate ahead of time. Investments like those implemented by both the Democrat president FDR and the Republican president Eisenhower brought forth the intangibles that helped make America the super power of the twentieth century.

American citizens will have to force that type of investment today though. Politicians do not have the will to resist their wealthy patrons and corporate masters. Any doubts Americans had of this should have been cleared up during the economic collapse of 2008. The bailout called Troubled Asset Relief Program or TARP strongly supported the troubled assets of banks. As banks and foreign investors were getting their principal amounts back dollar for dollar, average Americans were forced to grovel at the doorstep of the financial institutions. The same banks that had required taxpayer money to stay afloat were turning around and giving their benefactors the cold shoulder by denying loan modifications mandated by law.

Had there been any fairness at all in the system, then the credit card rates of Americans holding cards issued from TARP institutions should have been rolled back to rates equal to traditional usury laws. Usury laws, limiting interest rates on loans, were put in place many years ago to prevent loan sharking and extortion of money from people in difficult circumstances. In the late twentieth century, banks were made exempt from usury laws. They were considered responsible financial institutions and not loan sharks, so they received the exemption.

When it became clear that the banks were not responsible, this should have been the very first reaction. Immediately lifting the usury exemption for any financial institutions requiring TARP funds should have been done. Of course, no one in government offered it as an option. Banks were handed a business opportunity through the usury exemption in the late twentieth century. Citizens need not continue to grant the benefit to banks.

Admittedly, usury law is an obscure sector of the credit world, which sets low single digit interest rates as the only legal rate. Usury law seems quite archaic in today's world of twenty percent and higher interest rates. This is because BankAmericard and MasterCharge changed the credit landscape so dramatically in the seventies once the banks had received the usury exemption. The issuing of generic plastic credit cards in quantity put systemic structures in place that facilitated today's crisis.

As debt has grown in this country, banks have been able to generate quite a revenue stream from the interest rates on these large balances. Attempts at regulation of how interest rates are indexed, brings violent opposition from the industry. Regulation is met with threats to call in all the debt of Middle America as a response. The lack of adequate representation in government means that one of the big sticks, usury law, has never even been considered as a regulatory sanction against banks.

The point here is that Wall Street gets what it wants from Congress, but Main Street is ignored. Social Security and Medicare/Medicaid are NOT profitable. They represent the social contract between a nation and its citizens. Though, a case can be made that investments in these spaces are profitable over the extreme long view, they are not immediately profitable most of the time.

During the technological transition that has altered life so dramatically for the American worker, the comforting advice from Wall Street has been that the worker must bear down and learn new skills. The American worker must adapt in the twenty-first century to compete say the bankers. What has been good for the goose is now good for the gander says the libertarian-socialist. American banking must conform to a new twenty-first century regulatory regime.

Reining in the great casino of American banking is a requirement for a stable version of capitalism to continue in the twenty-first century.

Despite economic straits, libertarian-socialists know America must continue to spend for the future. The United States is still the largest economy in the world and the largest government budget in the world. America must invest in itself. Proper prioritization of that budget is essential to the future.

Building weaponry for the military never creates infrastructure. The defense of the nation is important without a doubt. However, the defense budget is one of the biggest threats to the nation's fiscal health. A recent audit of the Defense Department found that it had made unsupported journal entries totaling over six trillion dollars. This was only in 2015 and in just one of the service branches, the Army! The nation can no longer afford such loose accounting. Finding out where this money went would go a long way to bringing fiscal discipline to America's military.

Funding tax cuts to upper income brackets cannot be subsidized any longer. The United States cannot afford to stop spending, but it must be smart spending. Before the day of reckoning comes, the United States must invest in infrastructure and social support. These are the budget items that pay the big intangible dividends of the future. The unpredictable immeasurable dividends of investing in the right things are the game changers, when it seems like the game is lost.

Libertarian-Socialism understands that Americans supporting other Americans will cost money and lots of it. Libertarian-Socialism does not advocate profligate spending without check, though. The United States cannot ignore the debts as the nation makes these investments. America must deal with the debt before the creditors force it to do so. If the United States invests wisely now, it has a chance of being on the upturn economically when the fiscal day of reckoning comes. A stronger economy, publicly and privately, will give the United States the strength it needs to survive the economic hurricane on the horizon.

To invest in infrastructure and the citizenry over the longer term the United States must begin to pay down the debt. The interest rates on those debts make debt service one of the largest items in the American budget. More importantly though, an audit of day-to-day outflows must be undertaken to stop the debt from growing so rapidly. America cannot pay down any debts without understanding current outflows of cash.

Without too much digging, it is clear that a lot of money goes to far-flung areas of the globe. The size of American military obligations around the world is mind-boggling. It will take years to draw down these expeditionary forces deployed across the world. America's budgetary woes leave this nation no choice, but to draw down these foreign occupations. Until the nation does, it will continue to hemorrhage money at an incredible rate while doing nothing to build the American economy.

Additionally, post war veteran benefits are a poorly accounted future entitlement that will not be small. Libertarian-Socialists believe these military entitlements must be honored. The United States will be paying these promised entitlements for decades to come and the long-term cost has not been calculated. In short, there is a lot of debt and a lot of financial obligation baked into the future American budget, but very little unencumbered revenue to pay for it.

To start paying down the debt, the United States should institute a Value Added Tax (VAT). A VAT is essentially a national sales tax to create a new unencumbered revenue stream for the nation. A value added tax of a penny or two on each dollar will be applied evenly on all citizens. Given the multi-trillion dollar economy, a two-cent VAT could yield a trillion dollars to be applied against the debt in a few years.

For the VAT to be effective and to prevent revenue diversion as happened with Social Security, America must mandate by law that it goes to pay down the national debt. A large portion of that debt is held in the Social Security Trust Fund. The Social Security Trust Fund should be at the top of the list of items to be paid off by the VAT revenue.

As the United States pays the debts down to something manageable, Americans can then discuss real income tax reform. With stable revenue streams and reduced debt, income tax reform can be undertaken in a less hysterical environment. Americans can decide whether a VAT would be preferred over the current income tax.

There are many things to consider, such as whether the elimination of the mortgage interest deduction would destroy the housing market. This is just one of many big unknowns. The large increase in the standard deduction within the 2017 tax reform closes down access to the mortgage interest deduction and may negatively affect property values. Especially those homes that are too inexpensive to have the interest paid be enough to get the borrower over the standard deduction.

On the other hand, moderately expensive homes may actually increase even further and faster in value as the large mortgages generate interest payments large enough to cover the standard deduction and open up other write-offs on the Schedule A. This appears to be another example of a two-tiered system where the wealthy continue to enjoy the benefits of a government protecting their interests, while the less wealthy are exploited as an unimportant constituency.

Libertarian-Socialism can support significant tax reform, but it must be real and concrete. Reform requires locking down an honest accounting of revenue outflows at the Treasury, facilitating alternative revenue streams and paying down the debt obligations. Before putting these items in place wholesale income tax reform seems unwise, hence the libertarian-socialist's preference for a VAT before moving forward on big changes to the existing revenue streams are contemplated.

Running a government and a nation for profit, as many extreme capitalists advocate, does not benefit the greatest number of citizens. Tax revenue should be applied to the greater good. Nations as envisioned by the libertarian-socialist are to be run more like a family than a business. In a transparently run representative republic, the greater good is debated openly. Together in open debate the nation can arrive at what the greater good represents. In America's corporatist government, the greater good is defined by the bottom line of a narrow elite and their accountants, not by open and transparent debate.

A VAT will bring large amounts of money into government. It is almost guaranteed to succeed at righting America's financial ship given the size of the American economy. Guaranteed to work if the revenue is handled responsibly for the common good. In all things libertarian-socialist, responsible governance in conjunction with citizen engagement are absolute requirements for true success.

The twenty-first century has seen a number of exotic funding methods to finance the wars in Iraq and Afghanistan. Something known as "off budget" suddenly became a possibility in the American legislature when considering the War on Terror. The 2008 financial crisis did significant damage to America's balance sheet. The Federal Reserve's quantitative easing program amounts to printing money as well.

Common sense dictates that such profligate spending cannot continue indefinitely. The libertarian half of the patriotic libertarian-socialist understands there is a limitation even if one is the world's reserve currency. However, the socialist half recognizes that important investments can be done "off budget", if the society deems the effort worthy.

Achieving an Auditable Election System

Libertarian-Socialism recognizes that political progress cannot happen when elections are in such a turmoil. If voting results are not verifiable, then getting citizen engagement is futile as moneyed power controls the outcome in the end. Control of the ballot box forces elected officials to serve the interests of those that control the tallying of votes. Corruption becomes the status quo, because one must participate to get elected.

The representative republic is broken in a fundamental way when corruption is the politician's chief constituent. With so much power up for grabs every four years, there is no wonder that moneyed power would attempt to control elections. Honest elections encourage hard work by politicians, so that when the elections are held there are concrete accomplishments for voters to support.

Making leadership stand for election periodically is really the only tangible power average citizens possess. This relationship between honest elections and good governance has existed since ballot boxes and representative government began. It is not perfect by any means, but open elections at least give citizens a chance to remove politicians from leadership positions. Ultimately, the inherent selfishness of the political personality means they do not serve citizens without the threat of being removed from power.

The political duopoly of the Republican and the Democrat is very much a part of the electoral problems in the United States of America. The founding fathers never envisioned the amount of influence political parties hold over the American election process. Public money is used to run intra-party primaries in support of the duopoly.

The influence of parties is used by moneyed power to block "unsponsored" legislation, which make no profits for shareholders. Political parties continue to survive by serving moneyed power. Political parties exist almost solely to deliver legislation. Moneyed power pays for election results and supports the party structures for this reason.

The parties use this duopoly every ten years by leveraging the census to control elections. Politicians draw districts that guarantee one party or the other controls a seat, otherwise known as a gerrymander. As noted in the lost article of the Bill of Rights, Congressional districts should be redone after every census. Instead of the objective analysis of population distribution and seat expansion imagined by the founders, the parties invest their resources into demographic analysis to draw districts in favor of a particular party. Gerrymandering ensures that candidates must participate in the duopoly to compete, since no districts are gerrymandered to favor independents or third parties.

Gerrymandering makes districts far less representative of their constituents and creates divisive legislators hailing from partisan districts. The growing efficiency of software to gerrymander a political district, especially at the House of Representative level, helps cement these divisions. With ever more computing power and data granularity, code can be written allowing political strategists to draw districts that create just the right demographic to guarantee their bosses get re-elected.

There is no other way to explain the biennial ninety-eight percent reelection rate. This reelection rate stands in stark contrast to Congressional approval ratings in the thirty percent range or lower. These so-called "safe" districts have helped widen the bipartisan divide by virtually eliminating moderate, blended, centrist districts.

Libertarian-Socialism calls for the reining in of the software-driven gerrymandering that divvies up the electorate for the two parties. Through an objective analysis of population distribution within the United States, Congressional district lines should be limited to first honor current civic divisions at the local level before radical redrawing would be allowed. This means that a district would not likely cut through five or more cities, but rather adhere more closely to the existing civic boundaries.

Currently, in some districts, citizen voters of a small city may be represented by the same mayor, but forced to vote in one of three or four different congressional districts. This condition can occur even though they are living on the same city block. Of course, an expansion of the House of Representatives as discussed earlier would significantly reduce the importance of geographic factors. An increase in the number of Congressional districts results in decreasing of district size and makes gerrymandering more difficult.

Limiting gerrymandering will have a profound effect. Politicians are forced to advocate positions that are more moderate when their district is more diverse. This will surely be helpful in ending gridlock. Citizens living in the same neighborhoods might now also have a unified voice in Congress, instead of having their unified voice diluted at the federal level.

Nonetheless, no matter how fairly a district is drawn, if citizens choose not to cast a thoughtful ballot then there can be no fix. There is nothing that can substitute for an engaged electorate. When a plurality of Americans choose to identify as neither Democrat nor Republican, there is obviously a growing discontent with the duopoly. Gerrymandering is being used to protect the duopoly from this grassroots rebellion against political parties.

Technology has brought greater efficiencies to voting, but not brought about any transparency that enhances trust. Belief that the will of the electorate is being executed at the ballot box is at an all-time low. A lack of certainty in the outcomes by the electorate is discouraging and makes it harder to get citizens to the polls. Technology is used to increase certainty in the financial world, but in the election world technology has facilitated hacking,

Technology has further called into question the honesty of American elections. The 2000 election was dominated by hanging chads in Florida before the Supreme Court ruled Gore had lost. This disputed election led to a push for more computerized voting. The justification was supposed to be greater certainty in election results through technology as occurred in the financial world decades ago.

The next election was not one of greater certainty for the

electorate, however. In 2004, there was a huge discrepancy between exit polling and the election outcomes. There were specific irregularities in the Ohio counts that brought scrutiny to the computerized voting machines mandated after the 2000 election. In 2004, it became clear that the electronic systems had very little in the way of audit trails and monitoring mechanisms. Audit trails are necessary to facilitate transparent tallying of the votes while protecting the system from hacking.

The 2000 election was used to accelerate adoption of computerized voting machines. The 2000 election turmoil was a harbinger of future shenanigans in the twenty-first century. When Florida was in dispute in 2000, the Electoral College did not weigh in at all. At a time, when the architects of the nation would have expected the Electoral College to step in the institution yielded to the Supreme Court. This disputed election battle seemed to drive the oligarchy to gain more certain election outcomes that technology can deliver.

The Electoral College solution favored Gore who only needed one more electoral vote to become president, while Bush needed all of Florida's twenty-seven votes. The Electoral College had no real role in 2000. Instead, five men, several of them friends of the man standing for Vice President, Dick Cheney, decided the election. In the end, the Supreme Court installed George W. Bush to office even though he had lost the popular vote to Al Gore.

The 2000 election led to a large-scale push for computerized voting instead of a debate on why five men on the Supreme Court had swung an entire election. Why had the Electoral College not been the forum to decide the 2000 election? Why had the election not been thrown to Congress as had been done in previously contested elections where the electors could not decide? Authentic debate concerning the 2000 election should have included consideration of previous elections where the outcomes were debated in Congress.

Elections in history such as Thomas Jefferson over Aaron Burr in 1801, John Quincy Adams over Andrew Jackson in 1825 and Rutherford B. Hayes over Samuel Tilden in 1877 should be common knowledge to all Americans now had the proper public debate occurred. These were all elections where the Electoral College failed to arrive at a decisive result. Instead of discussions about the proper flow of decision-making powers in a disputed election, voting machines were advocated as solving the problems seen in 2000. The machines were adopted in many states across the country as a response to the controversial 2000 election result.

The election results delivered in 2004 after large-scale conversion to computerized voting are hardly a convincing case for computers over paper. In the presidential election of 2004, the discrepancies in exit polling to computer tallies were enormous. In New Mexico, which was decided by six thousand votes in the 2004 election, malfunctioning machines mysteriously failed to register properly a presidential vote on more than twenty thousand ballots. In Ohio, an electronic machine in the town of Gahanna recorded over four thousand votes for Bush and little over two hundred for Kerry. In that precinct, however, there were only eight hundred registered voters. Exit polling differences of this magnitude triggered Ukraine's Orange Revolution in 2003 and 2004. Sadly, in America complacency ruled the day.

Common Dreams, the news and opinion website outlines some of the discrepancies in the 2004 election as follows:

> *The evidence is especially strong in Ohio. In January, a team of mathematicians from the National Election Data Archive, a nonpartisan watchdog group, compared the state's exit polls against the certified vote count in each of the forty-nine precincts polled by Edison/Mitofsky. In twenty-two of those precincts -- nearly half of those polled -- they discovered results that differed widely from the official tally. Once again -- against all odds -- the widespread discrepancies were stacked massively in Bush's favor: In only two of the suspect twenty-two precincts did the disparity benefit Kerry. The wildest discrepancy came from the precinct Mitofsky numbered "27," in order to protect the anonymity of those surveyed. According to the exit poll, Kerry should have received sixty-seven percent of the vote in this precinct. Yet the certified*

tally gave him only thirty-eight percent. The statistical odds against such a variance are just shy of one in 3 billion. Such results, according to the archive, provide 'virtually irrefutable evidence of vote miscount.

The 2004 election put many technologists on alert. There was more activism from the technology sector. Organizations like Black Box Voting pushed for more transparency in the software collecting votes in the United States. Additionally, the lack of an audit trail was a clear shortcoming to even the most technologically naive. Nonetheless, in 2008, there were more anomalous election results.

In 2008, the American economy was in free fall. It was self-evident that the next president would be a Democrat. Hillary Clinton looked to be a lock in 2008 until Barack Obama upset the apple cart. Obama won the critical Iowa Caucuses opening the Democratic primaries with Clinton finishing third. Polling showed Obama was leading in the upcoming New Hampshire primary. However, when the votes were tallied Hillary Clinton had won New Hampshire.

Election analysts were on alert this time though. There were already many technologists looking closely at election results in 2008 after what had happened in 2004. It did not take long before someone surfaced the fact that Obama had won in hand counted districts in New Hampshire. The only districts where Clinton won were machine-tabulated districts. To add to the anomaly, the hand counted districts where Obama won matched leading polling. The hand counted districts matched exit polling that was done in New Hampshire while the machine tabulated districts swung wildly toward Clinton against the exit polls.

These results were so odd one wonders why more was not made of them. There was enough scrutiny that this discrepancy was at least reported. There were no more computerized anomalies reported in 2008. Could Barack Obama have been the Democratic nominee for president without New Hampshire's unusual voting tallies being surfaced to a wide audience?

Off and on since the insecurity of the 2000 and 2004 elections, American voting equipment occasionally gets some airtime, but for the most part attention has been elsewhere. Polling suggested there was little chance for Mitt Romney in 2012 and the popular vote echoed these polls. The Electoral College though appeared much closer and—had Ohio swung to Romney – Obama may have been a one-term president.

The hacking group Anonymous claims to have blocked a 2012 effort in Ohio to flip votes and swing the election. The claim was picked up by several news sources after the election. In hindsight, Karl Rove's candid facial reactions when Fox News calls Ohio for Obama would seem to lend some credence to the claim. Frankly, there is such a lack of audit trails in the American voting systems that the truth cannot be known.

In 2016, the popular vote diverged again from the Electoral College as Donald Trump became president and claims emerged of "hacking" that put Trump in office. Interestingly, all these recent claims of hacking are mostly about Russia or other foreign actors planting fake news stories in the American press and social media. This hardly amounts to hacking. This is simple propaganda and has been done since time immemorial.

If the Russians have the power to hack American elections, they may very well be taking advantage of purposeful holes put in the computerized voting machines to achieve a result by the duopoly. It seems that in a hyper-partisan environment, patriotism goes out the window. Both sides are willing to pay for a "fix" at any cost. The Russians are smart and most likely took money from both sides to hack. The losing side still does not want to expose the true insecurity of American elections to protect and preserve the duopoly.

In the twenty-first century, there have been these anomalous elections. In these elections the losing side realizes they have been had and the election swung. The rules do not change though, because delivering election outcomes is the reason political parties exist today. The duopoly treats the election manipulations as a game of political gotcha, where the side best able to master technology wins the day. With a wink and a nod of respect to the wiliness of their opponent, the duopoly will never advocate transparency. Transparent elections would dilute the power of the parties, end the duopoly's game of technological one-upsmanship and curtail the auctioning off of American legislative bodies.

Software has been a part of the American financial machinery for decades and there is no excuse for such a vulnerable election process. These vulnerabilities preserve the ability to deliver results regardless of the will of the electorate. Using technology to win elections is nothing new. The political party apparatuses are not as technologically challenged as they claim to be. This feigned ignorance is used to excuse these election process loopholes. Such claims of ignorance hold no water in light of the leveraging of technology in other areas of electioneering.

In 2016, the reluctance of the Democrats to take up the cause of the recount demonstrated how neither side would work toward a transparent election process. The Greens surprisingly were able to raise sufficient funds for recounts in several states compelling Democrats to pretend to support the recounts or bring down the curtain on election theatrics. Cynically, Democrats did not defend the recounts. When Republicans sought to cancel or limit the recounts, the Democrats did not show up in court to push back. Democratic inaction led directly to a curtailment of any extensive recounts in 2016. America can no longer ignore the fact that its elections are neither secure nor auditable.

All is not lost, though. Also in 2016, there was a successful push to force the retention of ballot images by the government and to make those images public. In Arizona, an election integrity advocate, John Brakey, requested ballot images from Pima County, and was told the images were being destroyed. Brakey sought and obtained a temporary restraining order to prohibit Arizona officials from destroying the images. It is this methodology that distills down to fundamental steps to force some transparency into the election system. This simple three-part method (ballot images, unique ID, public right to examine actual ballot images), are the three legs to an election transparency stool.

These three items make up the basis of election transparency because firstly, ballot images are already available with most voting systems; secondly, ballot images are already clearly included by precedent in the Freedom of Information rulings of most jurisdictions; finally, and perhaps most importantly, it costs little or nothing to implement the simple three-part method. This method is sometimes referred to as the Brakey method. It represents a real way to inject transparency into the election process when computerized voting machines are being used.

On top of this method, if a unique id or QR code is briefly displayed at the time of voting to the voter, it becomes extra powerful in the twenty-first century, since the voter could retain the unique identifier. In the privacy of the voting booth, the voter can quickly snap an image of that unique identifier. It makes it possible later for the populace to crowd source an audit of the vote. This is a very important check on the many possible ways to game voting.

Only voters would be able to tie their unique identifier back to *their* vote. Once the individual ballot images are available and retrievable by unique identifier, the threat of an audit makes it much more difficult to swing elections electronically. This makes the Electoral College so important to preserve. There is much talk of the Electoral College being a problem due to its mismatch to the popular vote. The reality is that the Electoral College is alerting citizens to the gaming of the elections.

The statistical improbabilities of the occurrences in American elections this century strain credulity. The Electoral College helps illustrate this fact by showing the large divergence between the popular vote and the Electoral College outcome. The duopoly will want to destroy the Electoral College, so that simply gaming the popular vote is all it takes to get into the White House. The districts of the Electoral College represent separate discrete, auditable units that can expose election hacking. No wonder that the duopoly would like to eliminate the Electoral College.

The Brakey Method makes auditable counts for elections a real possibility, but there is more to elections. For example, the questions of who can vote in an election and who did vote are not answered by the Brakey Method, which only produces transparency and auditability of the count. Even if the first two questions have answers that are of unquestioned veracity, the chain of custody remains a concern. Are the ballots and the images authentic? Have any gone missing or been added? Nonetheless, transparency and auditability of the count are powerful checks on election hacking. The Brakey Method is a fundamental reform advocated by libertarian-socialism.

The ground is as fertile as it ever has been for a new citizen-centric agenda to grab the support of the real Silent Majority. The programs that make up the social safety net, (Social Security, Medicare, Medicaid, Unemployment Insurance and eventually a single payer healthcare system) are a threat to the tax system that the oligarchy has been manipulating for decades.

In the United States, this tax system has brought three-quarters of the income growth to the wealthy. Moneyed power wants to preserve the status quo of the oligarchy and they have the means to pay for elections results. America's institutions have been hamstrung, preventing the representative republic from functioning as it should. To repair it, auditable elections are the only way to implement change in a nation hijacked by a greedy agenda.

Finally, if Americans do not get satisfaction on the computerized voting front, they should demand paper ballots. Paper ballots are not perfect, but they require a close election for the results to be gamed. The fact that the ballots exist in the physical universe makes adding to the counts logistically more difficult if the election is not a close one. It takes a lot more fake ballots to be produced when one side is polling below forty percent to swing an election. Digital swinging of elections does not require any closeness between the rivals. Computerized voting allows for HUGE swings of votes from one side to the other.

This nation used paper before and could do so again. When all else fails paper ballots and ink on our fingers can serve to produce election results that are more verifiable. Citizens can be a lot more confident about the results of a nationwide election when every precinct is using paper. Perhaps the next presidential election should be done with paper ballots. It may be the only way programs that support the citizenry as a whole will ever be implemented.

Libertarian-Socialism

The preceding chapters document that libertarianism and socialism have valid ideas to be applied to the nation's political culture. The universe of politically viable solutions shrinks when limited to one or the other. It is the blending that brings about a wealth of options and solutions. It may seem like political alchemy, but libertarian-socialism is real. It is a practical point of view. It is the fires of partisan discord along the left/right axis, which obstruct this synergy.

Solutions will come from both sides. The conversation between the patriotic libertarian and the patriotic socialist seeks to facilitate the participation of both sides. This is the core of libertarian-socialism. The libertarian-socialist vision of American politics seeks to re-ignite natural synergies by recreating the multi-polar political tension that once made American politics functional.

The liberal/conservative chasm that divides America, largely mirroring the Democrat/Republican fault line, has fractured the nation. Libertarian-Socialism can bridge the chasm of ideology. The conversation between the patriotic libertarian and the patriotic socialist shifts the paradigm from Democrat versus Republican back to America. The libertarian-socialist conversation is a direct threat to the wealth and power of the oligarchs.

The patriotic socialist and the patriotic libertarian often clash in their conversations about social programs. There is no doubt that there are differences here. However, there is agreement between the patriots that much of the aforementioned social experimentation based upon the softer sciences was heavily curtailed under Ronald

Reagan. The last remnants were effectively ended when Bill Clinton signed his austere welfare reform in the early nineties.

Most Americans do not realize that the Clinton welfare reform in the early nineties ended most of the real abuses of the system. This dramatic reduction of social support occurred in a little over a decade. It is baffling to hear shock jock radio deejays still shriek about such abuses today almost thirty years after these enormous cutbacks in the nation's social safety net. Stories of drug addicts getting disability and welfare queens collecting thousands by having babies are twentieth century artifacts. These narratives have nothing to do with the current state of affairs. They are now baked into the duopoly's talking points.

What follows are ideas that spring from the patriotic alliance of the libertarian and the socialist. Once you read about them, you will see how they are so very dangerous to moneyed power. Libertarian-Socialism is dangerous because it threatens these monopolies not through violent revolution, but with ideas so powerful, they change American behavior on Main Street.

Libertarian-Socialism seeks to bring unity instead of division to Main Street. Only united can Main Street find the strength to resist the powerful forces that divide the 99% into warring factions.

Reforming Our Broken Judiciary Branch

The Constitution is meant to be a living document and so it needs living stewards. That is why there is the Supreme Court and an amendment process, so it can be updated when needed. The amendment process is a high bar though, requiring a super majority of the state houses along with the normal legislative hurdles to federal law. This high bar is meant to encourage usage of the document in its simplest most original form without modification, but with interpretation.

This requires it to be arbitrated by the judicial branch, which is why there is a Supreme Court. The amendment procedure is supplemental to this judicial administration. The Constitution coupled with the amendment procedures provides a legal framework that a whole country can be based upon. However, the judicial branch dovetails the Constitution with the present. As the country's carpenters of legality, their lifetime appointments were meant to insulate them from politics.

The executive branch provides central leadership and decision-making to steer the ship of state. The legislative branch is to build a useful, relevant and just body of law on top of the constitutional framework to facilitate leadership and progress. As the world changes, the judicial branch balances the authoritarian nature of the executive branch and the reactive nature of the legislative branch with a longer view. The judiciary should be checking the politically driven unconstitutional outputs of the other two branches, but that has not been the case.

The Supreme Court's ability to interpret how the authors of the founding documents would rule in the twenty-first century has made its members quite powerful. Libertarian-Socialists understand that matters of money can breach this insulation of the judicial branch. This has led the judicial branch to become ever more politicized. It is hard to imagine anything more politicized than installing the president as the court did in 2000. Five judges decided who would be the first president in the 21st century. One of those five votes came from a man, Antonin Scalia, who was the hunting friend of the Republican vice-presidential candidate, Dick Cheney.

It is difficult to understand why Scalia did not recuse himself making it a four to four stalemate vote. Historical precedents indicated allowing the recounts to continue or for the election to go to the House as it had in previously disputed elections in the nineteenth century. Alternatively, the original intent of the Electoral College delegates was to break such a logjam before the Supreme Court should be involved. Those are two constitutional courses that the court appeared to block for political reasons not judicial ones in 2000. Scalia's choice to ignore those precedents has irreversibly changed the Supreme Court's role in the constitutional balancing act.

Partisans point to the fact that the Electoral College debate could not be considered, because George W. Bush required ALL 27 of Florida's electoral votes. The potential solution of weighting the Florida electoral votes by popular vote was never debated. If Bush only got thirteen or fourteen electoral votes as the Florida popular vote indicated, Al Gore wins. In fact, even if Bush got 95% of the popular vote giving him twenty-six of the twenty-seven electoral votes, Gore still won. The winner-take-all method was the only way there would be a Republican president to start the twenty-first century. It is these real and reasonable constitutional remedies that makes Scalia's failure to recuse himself seem even more obviously politically motivated.

One cannot ignore the devolution of the Supreme Court confirmation hearings since the eighties. Nowadays no ideas about the role of the Supreme Court and the judiciary in American life are being debated. Real legal issues of import are completely absent from the proceedings. The earlier Robert Bork confirmation did debate issues of how the Constitution would be interpreted in the modern era. When Bork was not confirmed for specific issues relating to how he interpreted the Constitution, the follow up nominee, Douglas Ginsberg turned out to have a past selling marijuana. That of course ruled him out and Anthony Kennedy was plucked from a California law school.

In retrospect, the Robert Bork confirmation hearings were a lot more like what one would expect and what the country requires from the confirmation hearing. The results were far more concrete and long lasting. Anthony Kennedy turned out to be a middle of the road moderate that actually acted as if he were independent of politics. The Senate's advise and consent role was effectively leveraged to prevent a Supreme Court judge from being seated based upon that individual's testimony about American law and the Constitution as well as his historical legal opinions. This is what happened to Robert Bork. It actually is how this process should work.

In the case of Anita Hill though, Democrats made very little effort to derail Clarence Thomas based upon his legal opinions. As a black Republican, Clarence Thomas presented a conservative face to a duopoly that pigeonholed him as a liberal due to his race. This was wrong, but liberal opposition to Thomas was hamstrung by their stereotypes. Rather than debating Thomas' legal opinions, the Anita Hill gambit was put forth. Despite a lot of lurid testimony, Clarence Thomas went on to be confirmed. The Brett Kavanaugh hearings followed the same model.

Libertarian-Socialists know that since the confirmation of Clarence Thomas, the court has become ever more political in its rulings. The politics of the members on the bench seems to color their decisions more than objective interpretation of the law. Clarence Thomas and his limited government philosophy should have made him the tie-breaking vote when the federal ban on growing marijuana for personal use made it all the way to the Supreme Court in the nineties.

The basic premise was that the federal ability to regulate marijuana was based upon the interstate commerce clause. If a citizen grew the plant for personal use, did not sell it and did not transport it, how could interstate commerce be a factor? Somehow, though, Clarence Thomas found a way to rule with other Republicans on the court to maintain the federal prohibition on growing marijuana.

Clarence Thomas ushered in an era of court rulings based upon political affiliations. Despite the fact that people of color were disproportionately being imprisoned in the War on Drugs, Clarence Thomas voted to continue the draconian prohibition of a plant at the federal level. It is politics on the Supreme Court that has caused it to stray from its objective mission.

Libertarian-Socialists understand the need for the judicial branch, but they also understand that corruptions of money and power have weakened the system. Citizens need to understand the laws more than ever, so as exercise their constitutional role to combat these corruptions. Constitutionally, the people are allowed to push back against judicial dictatorship through jury nullification. Understanding the constitutional framework of the nation can help the people lead the Supreme Court to the correct rulings. The people can help shape law by communicating what they see as the nation's judicial shortcomings.

Those judicial shortcomings are especially evident when it comes to an individual citizen's right to protections from intrusions by the state or moneyed power. The Fourth and Fifth Amendments clearly lay out the extent of the individual's right to privacy, though without using the word, privacy. This has led to the complaint that activist judges are making up law, because the word "privacy" does not appear in the Constitution or amendments.

Libertarian-Socialists recognize the world evolves as time goes by and the legal parlance of the day changes too. What did the founding fathers mean, when they wrote this: "*...the people to be secure in their persons, houses, papers, and effects, against unreasonable searches and seizures, shall not be violated...?*" Libertarian-Socialists believe there is a clear constitutional right to privacy defined here. The Supreme Court exists to interpret a concept like privacy in the twenty-first century and future centuries. Unfortunately, so far that interpretation has been deeply flawed in the libertarian-socialist's view.

Repeatedly, there are examples in the news of individual privacy rights being breached with no repercussions for those that breached them. For example, if proper constitutional protections were enforced, the strip search of a teenage girl for ibuprofen would not only be seen as a violation of privacy, but a grave violation of the basic tenants of human rights and child pornography laws. Nonetheless, just such a case made its way through America's broken justice system.

Common sense is scarce in American courts and such actions by middle school staff in the Safford Unified School District led to little more than a wrist slap for the overzealous do-gooders. The Savana Redding case went all the way to the Supreme Court, because local courts in Arizona found no illegal behavior in stripping a 13-year-old girl to search for ibuprofen. Though the Supreme Court eventually determined that the strip search of the teenage girl was unconstitutional, it shielded the district from liability claiming the law was not clearly established at the time the act was committed. Thus, no consequences befell the perpetrators of such an obvious violation of individual rights and liberty.

When a teenage girl's naked body cannot be protected by the Constitution and the Bill of Rights, what can be protected? American law has strayed from common sense. It is not justice when the Supreme Court shields agents of the state from obviously unconstitutional and illegal acts claiming such limits were not clearly defined. The Supreme Court's rulings no longer look like an objective balancing of the needs of the state and the needs of the individual. This is especially troubling in a time when the needs of the state are often defined by moneyed power.

Due to the lifetime nature of the appointments to the court, the political duopoly is being baked into the legal system. This has to stop. It has caused innumerable machinations in the nation's elections. The incredible power that the five robes have on the court has tipped the balance. As a nation, the United States needs an alternative to these lifetime appointments. With a term limit on the bench, the power of each appointment is reduced.

Libertarian-Socialists would support a finite term for a Supreme Court justice. A term of ten years, staggered among the nine justices, means that almost annually, there would be a chance for an appointment to the court. If we make the seat on the bench limited to two terms, then no justice will ever serve for more than twenty years. This will likely require an amendment to the Constitution, but the alternative model, as we have seen this century, leaves much to be desired.

National Service and the Student Loan Crisis

The student loan crisis is real. There are billions, upon billions of dollars of debt being dragged around by Americans, especially young Americans. The student loan, which seemed so useful to the economically challenged when it was created, has become a parasite on subsequent graduating classes. Tuition has accelerated beyond rates of inflation with more and more government money in the form of student loans ballooning tuition.

In the last two decades, college tuition has risen by two hundred percent while the total rate of inflation has been less than sixty percent over the same time period. This is a result of guaranteed government revenues injected into the open market. Raw socialism can cause unnatural inflation in any system when there is not adequate regulation on the market side.

Guaranteed student loans are a no-risk investment. This is encouragement for banks to make loans to students knowing the government will back the transactions if there is a default. Such guarantees of government backstopping risk has always had the inherent potential of creating a financial bubble. The Great Recession of 2008–09 was brought on by similarly easy-money loans on houses with government backstopping much of the risk.

Once the houses turned out to no longer be worth as much as was paid, the inherent insecurity of mortgage-backed securities became apparent and 2008 saw the collapse of financial markets. Similarly, as a college education is no longer a guarantee of a good job, the fact the price of tuition has increased so much makes little sense. Such diminishing returns means the student loan bubble probably ought to have burst already.

The reason the bubble has not burst in the student loan market is because the government has made it very difficult for people to avoid paying these loans back. Declaring bankruptcy does not get one out of paying one's student loans in the way one can do with a mortgage. You cannot walk away from a student loan the way you can a house.

It is patently unfair that these enormous balances are not subject to forgiveness under bankruptcy law. By exempting student loan debt from bankruptcy, the average student debtor is locked into decades of debt service. These individuals are unable to escape creditors through the courts. The alleged servants of the people, DC politicians, have instead served corporate and financial masters by exempting student loans from normal bankruptcy protections. In effect, politicians created and have maintained a citizen class chained into long-term indentured servitude.

Student loans represented easy money that Americans could throw at college educations. Like any system awash in money, academia became a sponge to soak up additional revenues in many different ways. The cost of a college education skyrocketed due to the artificial injection of easy money. This made the need for loans greater and a vicious circle of debt acquisition was initiated.

In 2016, Bernie Sanders' plan to forgive all student loan debt sounded fantastic to an army of Americans carrying around this special kind of debt burden. His rhetoric struck a chord. Sanders did not even have to talk about how to pay for such a debt forgiveness plan. All other candidates on both sides of the aisle had been continuing the squeeze. This is a pocketbook issue for many citizens, so Bernie Sanders was the only vote for them. No wonder Bernie Sanders did so surprisingly well against Hillary Clinton through most of the Democratic primaries in 2016.

However, libertarian-socialism does not allow for giving away something for nothing, because this has a deeply corrupting influence. This is doubly so when the "giving away" is directly attached to a politician's electability as in the case of Bernie Sanders. Though Sanders' central premise is correct, which is that the government can afford to pay for a college education, the patriotic libertarian and a patriotic socialist cannot agree upon such a direct subsidy.

Libertarian-Socialists understand that the reason the government can seem to have a bottomless bag of money is the power to print money through seigniorage privileges. The government has enormous revenues, but can also print fiat currency that is not backed by gold or other tangible commodity. That is how all the twenty-first century military adventures have been financed. So clearly, Sanders is correct that it is possible to do such things "off the books".

It is clear that easy money artificially raises costs within a given system. Higher education and the trillion dollar Defense Department budgets are perfect examples. The corrupting influences of such unchecked revenue streams are real and corrupting. Just as they have corrupted the Pentagon, they have corrupted academia. Adding more money as Sanders proposes seems unlikely to fix the problem.

Libertarian-Socialism recognizes that there are other measures of worth in this world than money. The military budget can grow so enormous because the "currency of national security" is so highly valued that almost any amount expended is seen as money well spent. Similarly, a college education has historically been seen as a lucrative employment guarantee, which itself is also a highly valued commodity. Unfortunately, that guarantee is no longer as certain in either case. In fact, the former case is precisely why the United States has a mountain of debt with little to show for it.

From a libertarian-socialist point of view, Sanders' plan to forgive all student loan debt and give away a college education to all Americans was a pipe dream and a disaster waiting to happen. If a college education is no longer a guarantee of a good job in this country, then it makes no sense to continue to throw large amounts of money at institutions that are not churning out the expected commodity with any consistency. One of the tenets of markets is that there has to be consequences for delivering a poor product. Sanders' program violates this basic principle.

Secondly, there are Americans that have paid back their student loans. There are in fact millions of Americans that have paid back all or significant portions of their student debt. It hardly seems fair that those that have paid back the loans should not get refunds, if others are getting their debt loads forgiven. Sanders' plan simply had not been thought through. It was a battle plan meant to win the war, which it nearly did. However, as a practical plan that meets the high standard of agreement between a patriotic American socialist and a patriotic American libertarian, Sanders' free college plan falls short.

Libertarian-Socialism does have a fairer plan with some checks and balances for subsidizing higher education. That plan revolves around a national service initiative. One year of national service tied to forgiving one year of tuition, up to $25,000, brings some balance to the Sanders' plan. The free college plan now can have some viability, because there is a vehicle for students to pay back their free tuition in an alternative medium of exchange, labor. Perhaps $25,000 is too generous or too stingy, but it is a place to start the conversation.

The nature of the National Service can be leveraged in many ways. It can be used to encourage training in certain professions at higher rates. The United States has many, many initiatives that could be buoyed by some kind of national service program. It certainly would engage citizens in the business of developing and managing the country. First-responders and other professions that America believes will be in demand in the future would have enhanced tuition reimbursement. For example, in the case of doctors Americans might subsidize a full year of tuition with nine months of national service. National service provides a new medium of exchange for the national treasury.

This remuneration of tuition for service can also be leveraged to bring a broader section of the society into military service. Military service, which already offers tuition reimbursement during or after service, should always have the highest tuition to service reimbursement rate. In the context of the aforementioned reimbursement details, a two to one ratio perhaps makes sense: six months of service equating a whole year of college tuition would be the practical effect. In addition, older mid-career veterans looking to relieve enormous debt loads could take advantage retroactively as well.

This kind of national service encouragement could be seen as a military draft. Any military draft is a complicated social initiative. Libertarian-Socialists do not consider a draft to necessarily be a bad thing for American society. In fact, the Germans consider the military draft an absolute necessity to prevent the rise of another group like the Nazis. A national service program in the US can accomplish the same goal of bringing diversity into the military ranks. In addition, it provides a new vehicle for relieving student loan debt.

America is becoming vulnerable to the dangers of a narrow military class. History has demonstrated the perils of this situation. The Nazi Party aligned itself with German military interests and over time, the all-volunteer German army was populated with a large number of Nazis. When Hitler came to power, the military supported his repeal of freedom and liberty, because they were all members of the same political party. A similar military/political alliance may be growing in the United States right now.

Libertarian-Socialists urge Americans to consider a compulsory national service from its young people. One year of national service before the age of thirty need not be that onerous. After this first year of service, subsequent years contribute to the citizen's "scholarship fund". In this plan, a one to one ratio of service to college tuition does not seem too generous is the view of most libertarian-socialists. Combining a solution for relieving student loan debt makes National Service more practical and broadens support for Sanders' core plan.

Such a national service program makes the declaration of war even more important and less likely as well. Compulsory National Service would put much of the nation's youth on the line, not just a particular social class, if the United States declares war. Compulsory national service puts a much broader cross section of society in harm's way. That larger cross section compels some debate in the legislature before going to battle.

Citizens would have some choice on how to serve. National service should not be solely a pipeline for the military branches. The "national servants" need not necessarily join an active branch of military. A national service program must recognize there are more ways to serve one's country than taking up arms. Certainly, there must be active and reservist military options, but also a non-military domestic service path. Something in the vein of the Depression-era Works Projects Administration or the Conservation Corps would have plenty of work to do on American infrastructure.

Those that choose an active military role would be just that, ACTIVE duty military, for at least a two-year hitch, but also immediately begin accumulation of the "scholarship funds". A year of tuition for six months of service means such a hitch could fund four years to a bachelor's degree. This is a bit better than the current G.I. Bill, which requires three years of service. This also allows for a retroactive G.I. Bill where graduates with large debt loads and poor job prospects can relieve their debts via national service, retroactively.

As a matter of national security, all national servants should receive the same basic training program as part of their entry into a national service initiative. Of course, any basic training program is going to include weapons training. National servants whether they join the military branches as part of their service or not, should be able to take up arms, if necessary. This is what a patriotic libertarian and a patriotic socialist will agree upon; all Americans will take up arms to defend the nation when the enemy is on the beaches, among the hedgerows and in the streets.

A national service program must deal with the worst case scenario where military action is required. The United States used to have a clear definition of what was "required" before military action and that was a formal declaration of war from the Congress. National service puts actions like the continuous Global War on Terror back into the Congressional debate.

National service really forces Americans to accept what is required to make war instead of endless "police actions". Those that choose a reservist role or the National Guard could only be called up to active military duty if a formal declaration of war is made in Congress. Those that choose a domestic alternative like the Conservation Corp or humanitarian role like Peace Corps, could still opt out of "active" military service, if war were declared. Libertarian-Socialists recognize this must be respected.

Having a national service program for America's youth also ensures that all segments of society have had some military or military-like training. This could actually prevent gun violence, because more and more civilians will have had weapons training as time goes on. Additionally, this would diminish the chance that the military becomes affiliated with just one political party, which is a tremendously dangerous situation as German history demonstrates.

Most importantly, America recognizes a new way for citizenry to serve in exchange for an education. This exchange must be clearly and transparently administrated with quick renumeration to be effective. There is now a tremendous chance for infrastructure projects to be tackled by a domestic work force paid in this new currency. A debtless future for our youth is a worthy goal.

Only the People Can Protect Privacy

Some have said that the right to privacy is a manufactured right and not specifically written into the Constitution. The claim that privacy cannot exist as an idea without the specific word is specious. Without a doubt the founding fathers meant for Americans to have privacy when they wrote, *"...the people to be secure in their persons, houses, papers, and effects, against unreasonable searches and seizures, shall not be violated..."* Libertarian-Socialists believe this defines a clear constitutional right to privacy.

From the very beginning, the founding fathers laid a framework for individual freedom that made established power uncomfortable. That discomfort grew with how strong the framework proved in the protection of individual liberty. Despite the efforts of moneyed power, little could be done in nineteenth century America to deconstruct this framework without declaring martial law. The land was so vast and movement so easy that keeping track of citizens was a crap shoot at best. Politicians struggled to even come up with laws that COULD restrict individual liberty in any practical real world way.

The twentieth century saw the government begin to pass more laws that made individual privacy a secondary consideration in affairs between the state and the individual. Nonetheless, a modicum of privacy remained for the individual due to technical surveillance limitations of the time. In fact, well into the second half of the twentieth century, technology limits kept a lot of private information, actually private. The desires of power to make it otherwise were limited by the cost of computers, the lack of storage capacity, and slower processor speeds.

The close of the twentieth century saw rapid technological

development as the scene and Moore's Law turned out to be quite accurate. By the time that the planes ran into the Twin Towers privacy had already suffered serious abridgment. The 9/11 terrorist attacks sent the last vestiges of privacy out the window. Fear drove a massive expansion of police powers in this country. Driven by fear, most Americans were happy to be searched at the airport and elsewhere.

The radical freedom-loving founding fathers of the eighteenth century would be truly appalled at the twenty-first century government intrusion into individual privacy. Expectations of privacy in the modern era have been eroded beyond all recognition to even twentieth century eyes, let alone the eyes of the radicals that formed the United States of America. For centuries in the United States, expectations of privacy were quite high, even in public spaces. Since the World Trade Center attacks, those expectations have been curtailed significantly. Most modern Americans believe the loss of privacy is a requirement for safety and accept it as unavoidable.

Government, law enforcement, and corporate interests today have vast stores of data on people. Many citizens are mostly unaware of how much data is available on demand about them. Frankly, even if people were aware, they could do little to control the distribution of the data. The government and corporate interests wish to preserve their ability to monitor the citizenry and their customers. The government has entered into a disturbing alliance with technology companies to protect and expand this ability. Google, Facebook, Verizon, Amazon and others all have government contracts to facilitate the surveillance that is part of the Patriot Act.

Libertarian-Socialism opposes the unconstitutional spying being done in this country. This activity is allegedly done in the interests of public safety and to protect Americans from terrorists. As a practical matter, it is too often exploited by the moneyed and powerful to protect their interests. As a result, the privacy of an individual American citizen has devolved significantly. Individual liberty has been eroded and leveraged by the moneyed and powerful to keep them in money and in power. However, public safety has not been enhanced.

The United States is founded on privacy and personal security for the individual. Without this personal privacy, America ceases to be America. As from the preamble,"...*securing the blessings of liberty for ourselves and our posterity*" means that as technology changes, the same high bar of privacy that was established by the eighteenth century founders is the type of privacy to be sought by the twenty-first century citizen. Privacy is clearly one of the true blessings of individual liberty. Of course, it is more difficult in this digital age of data mining and cameras on every street corner, but achieving a real balance on the personal privacy front is a prerequisite to freedom.

Largely unsaid and unconsidered in this debate is the fact that so much data is generated by the average citizen in the course of an average day that it no longer became necessary to actually implement an overt or covert surveillance regime. A surveillance society simply evolved organically through technological advancement. Following the commission of any crime, law enforcement is immediately able to access security cameras, cell phone records and countless other sources of personal data to verify alibis. This much surveillance should have created a safer society, but it does not seem to have done so. Additionally, libertarian-socialists believe that with every person essentially in possession of a robot bodyguard in the form of a cell phone that the number of peace officers should have decreased. This has not happened and in fact, the opposite has happened.

There are many individuals and corporations making money with the data in addition to requirements of law enforcement. The implicit passive surveillance that has evolved should justify an increase in everyday freedom, but it has not. It is hard to imagine that actual privacy could ever return without an enormous grassroots push to get there. The corporations using this consumer data represent a large and powerful special interest group. This special interest group makes less money on privacy and might be a greater obstacle to privacy than the anti-terrorism fear-mongers.

Rather than allowing more and more surveillance by government, law enforcement and corporate interests, America needs to curtail it. The data footprints that everyone leaves these days are sufficient to reconstruct a person's actions on any given day. Instead of providing more surveillance powers to the authorities, the United

States should provide individual citizens with a "privacy firewall" that law enforcement, the government and corporations cannot pierce without court intervention. This is essential in the new century.

Libertarian-Socialism believes that freedom and privacy for individuals invigorates society rather than putting it at risk. The surveillance society stifles innovation and threatens individual freedom. A faith in freedom is not as difficult as the peddlers of fear would have Americans believe. Americans once had a deep understanding that giving up too much personal freedom was tantamount to giving up control of their lives. Looking past fear, somewhere deep down in all Americans there is still this common sense idea about personal control that once was a hallmark of the average American's worldview. Libertarian-Socialism seeks to tap this dormant worldview. America should be the Home of the Brave, not the Hovel of the Fearful.

That same American common sense recognizes that multi-billion dollar corporations are going to protect their income streams. That means not only will they act as a special interest group opposing increased individual privacy, they are likely to use the data for more than just marketing. Corporate spying is a cost of doing business for most and they can be very motivated to derail any market-breaking invention. A lack of privacy in a surveillance society means those with power can monitor those without power for possible disruptive innovations. However, it may be government regulation that motivates them more than anything else. After all, corporations don't need to concentrate on each other, they can turn the surveillance tools onto politicians that they need to vote a certain way.

Corporations with the right connections and sufficient money can watch rivals more easily than the average citizen might think. Mark Zuckerberg is one of the wealthiest men on the planet and his company knows a lot about many people. Imagine what happens to his business model in the libertarian-socialist vision of privacy.

Revenue streams based upon watching consumers are billions of dollars annually. Make no mistake, the rich and powerful protect their revenue streams. If Facebook's business model is challenged, there will be push back. It may come under the guise of national security and not corporations protecting their revenue streams, but the push back will be there. The true motivations of such sponsored legislation would not be national security, but the protection of a business model and the money it delivers.

The connection between corporate intelligence networks and intelligence agencies of nation states has become so close that the distinctions hardly make sense any longer. It can be hard to see where private intelligence networks end and nation state networks begin. The CIA even admits to allowing current CIA agents to moonlight for corporate interests. The CIA confirms the practice in a surprisingly unapologetic fashion.

Powerful, corporate interests pay for results, not constitutional obstacles. The CIA and NSA have access to all kinds of digital back doors to privacy as confirmed by Edward Snowden, WikiLeaks, et al. Corporations pay well for access to such back doors, no doubt. Lack of privacy is bad for America and surely stifles growth and innovation. The libertarian-socialist understands that individuals do have a right and a need to protect data collected about them.

There is more to consider than just the monetary aspects of this lack of privacy, of course. When the government can monitor dissenters so easily and completely, there is a very real, chilling effect across the whole of society. As cages are rattled in the halls of power, the databases are opened and mined for information to protect the powerful. Politicians will always use this data to quash dissent and political competition. Getting incriminating or just embarrassing information on a rival in an election can mean the difference between winning and losing. A crusading politician that threatens the moneyed and powerful can be easily controlled and, if necessary, rendered impotent in this century.

To preserve the intent of the founding fathers when it comes to privacy, citizens must own the data collected about them. It is impractical to pass laws that prevent the data being collected. Imagining that the data will not be collected, because of statute is naive. The data exists and will be collected, if for no other reasons than to *secure the blessings of convenience* in the 21st century digital age. Libertarian-Socialism does not begrudge the rich and powerful their revenue streams, but individual privacy is the only way to level the playing field.

Billing data, banking data, movement data, communication data, buying patterns, et cetera, will be collected in the future as they are now. To give individuals the requisite privacy, the law of the land must force "initial anonymization" of this data. The power to decrypt and "de-anonymize" the collected data remains with the individual...OR the courts when necessary through that pesky tedium, due process of law. The individual owns the "keys to their kingdom", but the private key for decryption is put in a public escrow repository.

The laws need to require encryption to prevent easy access to the data without keys. Those encryption keys should be in control of the citizen who owns the data with an escrowed key used for decryption, but which must be obtained through the courts and the owners of the data notified. Additionally, individuals should have encryption technologies that prevent the searching of their personal computers without a warrant. The howls from law enforcement can drown out all reason, but Americans are innocent until proven guilty. Recent court cases have compelled individuals to give up passwords for such encryption technologies, but this would seem to be a clear violation of the Fifth Amendment.

Those with their hands on the levers of power will always use fear to stop the push for individual privacy. There will always be bank robbers, kidnappers, pedophiles, and other horrific individuals who will use the tools of technology to their own nefarious ends in the same way that guns and knives can be used. Repeatedly, Americans are faced with the basic premise of a nation created by the founding fathers, which elevated the individual above the state or at least equal to the state. The founding fathers embraced the concept of allowing ninety-nine guilty defendants go free rather than imprison one innocent person. Privacy is required to achieve that goal.

The loss of privacy in the twenty-first century erodes the rights of individuals and compels scared citizens to give away what remains of their rights to the detriment of the rest. Only through court actions, subpoenas, search warrants, and the like, should the escrow key decryption be applied. This overrides the individual's privacy using the public repository of private decryption keys. Individuals should always be informed when their data is subpoenaed, because the private data on an individual is indeed their private data.

Protecting individual data and privacy from the government

and law enforcement is necessary for obvious reasons, but those same restrictions need to apply to the corporate data miners too. Legislation should be sending powerful messages in the privacy laws that will force corporate owners of personal data to "anonymize" and provide encryption of this data by the key chosen by the owner. Only a groundswell of support from the grassroots can force lawmakers to pass such laws.

A lack of individual liberty cripples positive change. Libertarian-Socialism endeavors to reinstate the modicum of privacy Americans once enjoyed in the past. Through the jury and court system people can roll back these abuses of official power. An upwardly mobile meritocracy is the positive outcome that true privacy brings to the societies that have the courage to embrace it.

The laws will need real teeth, and corporations, government officials or individuals that violate them must face severe penalties. Penalties that have serious repercussions will be required, or the potential positive effect on the bottom line by leveraging personal data will be too difficult to resist. Juries must punish corporate violators so that the private sector truly fears entering the courtroom on charges of "trafficking in personal data."

For example, social media companies control a lot of data about individual habits. Any breaches on their part of data anonymization could be penalized by enforcing multi-year fines indexed on gross revenues. Such revenue-based penalties would seriously punish a data privacy violator. Imagine the pain and suffering to the companies' bottom lines when they fail to protect privacy. Corporations will comply with these restrictions, especially if juries punish them repeatedly for not doing so. Over time, they will comply.

Government on the other hand will continue to push their overarching right to act in the national security interest. Corporations will support this push as a way to circumvent the punishments in the courtroom. The United States government is no longer used to the idea of individual rights trumping the rights of the federal authority. The United States government believes that it has the power to wiretap all communications in the country, and so far, no court has ruled against them. Allowing the government to mine data at will is destructive to freedom. Nonetheless, corporations will use their resources to continue to allow unfettered data mining for the government and themselves.

The American Civil Liberties Union and Electronic Frontier Foundation started to pull back the curtain on these domestic spying issues through their lawsuits against the telephone companies that aided and abetted the Bush Administration's surveillance escalation in 2001 before the twin towers attacks. Unfortunately, the Obama administration helped shutdown these lawsuits by granting immunity to the telecommunication companies that had cooperated with the unconstitutional wiretapping ordered by Bush. The politicians will not protect individual privacy. Politicians will protect corporations from legal repercussions until their constituents loudly require a different outcome.

Citizen awareness of government actions will be the first steps toward elevating individual privacy again in this country. It is only the first step, because the federal government holds many cards in the game. In 2001, the United States government offered the telecommunication companies about $10,000 per wiretap when it embarked on its wiretapping regimen. The phone companies saw a big revenue stream, once they realized how extensive the government domestic spying program was going to be, so they complied.

All telecommunication companies complied, *except* for a company called Qwest. Qwest refused on constitutional grounds. The company was rewarded for its patriotism by the cancellation of government contracts that it had already secured. Of course, the owner could see his stock price was going to fall in this battle, and he ended up selling some of his shares quite logically. The government tried and convicted him for insider trading. He went to prison. The chilling effect was very real.

Once the Qwest CEO, Joe Nacchio got out of jail in 2014, he hinted that his arrest and conviction were directly related to his non-cooperation with the NSA. The holders of power want this information to be known to control others, so his words are allowed. In some ways, this CEO's story mirrors that of Mikhail Khodorosky, a billionaire that was jailed for tax evasion in Russia. Most understood Khodorosky's jail time was due to opposing ex-KGB agent, Vladimir

Putin, in an allegedly open election. Authoritarian-capitalism is a real thing and it is on the march across the globe.

The government is in a position to either bribe or bully a corporation into complying. It should be obvious to the libertarian-socialist that courtroom rebukes brought by free juries are the only path. It is foolish to believe that the data miners are going to concentrate on protecting citizens when there are so many other profitable uses for the data. Besides the government encourages and wants them to do this collection and data mining. Libertarian-Socialists will have to work hard to bring privacy back to America.

Libertarian-Socialists should ask questions like, "With all this surveillance power, what was the SEC up to at the beginning of this century? They obviously were not watching AIG and the rest of the financial robber barons as a financial collapse was looming."

Libertarian-Socialists should ask, "Why with the level of data mining going on how did Bernie Madoff make off with billions, while Martha Stewart landed in prison?"

Libertarian-Socialists should ask, "Why was Martha Stewart so important to prosecute, while the entire banking system was being looted?" Libertarian-Socialists can postulate that perhaps she annoyed a powerful person at a powerful gathering. The SEC was used to punish her disrespectful behavior. The above scenarios would be predicted outcomes of corporate and government snooping. This is precisely how decreased privacy and increased surveillance makes Americans less safe.

Without individual privacy, Americans lose their freedom and strength. Individuals become subject to all manner of harassment from petty government officials. Repeatedly, Americans can see private data being used for revenge and political or financial gain, not the preservation of justice. Individuals should understand that a government that does not respect individual privacy does not make them safer, but rather, it puts them at risk for revenge, persecution, and oppression of the worst kind.

The judges have not protected privacy for the individual any better than the politicians have. Only individual juries can begin to acquit defendants when the prosecution presents the "fruit of the poisoned tree" which is what unconstitutionally collected evidence represents. Only when people understand and take back their own privacy and then act on that understanding as conscientious citizens on juries can privacy be protected. This is another powerful reason for common sense libertarian-socialists to support jury rights. Common sense tells libertarian-socialists that change will not come from the holders of the power.

How Americans Came to Distrust Science

Americans have devolved from one of the most rationally, scientific people on the planet to one of the most distrustful of science. Libertarian-Socialism recognizes that this is a dangerous and untenable situation. Science is the basis of the modern world. It cannot be rejected, because it does not adhere to a political agenda. Like everything in America, politics and money has polluted science and corrupted it.

The world finds it difficult to grasp the American scientific devolution from most rational to one of the least rational nations on earth. It is especially baffling for those on the outside looking in after the United States had been instrumental in marshaling global support for environmental laws to curtail pollution. American environmental law founded in hard scientific data, became the basis of global law implemented at the United Nations.

A coalition of environmentalists and scientists got traction in the middle of the last century pointing out the fragility of the global environment. They sounded the alarm on industrial and agricultural pollution. Rachel Carson's book Silent Spring had a large impact on opinion as it related to pesticide use. Of course, the deadly smog choking large cities like London got people's attention as well. Prevention of ozone layer destruction was also clearly a political movement based on real scientific data. Scientists were correct to make common cause with politicians and social engineers on these issues.

These regulations on air pollution and water pollution often collided with private property rights. Scientists were key in winning legislative battles proving that the natural systems were connected.

The data supported claims that pollution on private property could threaten public health. Unhoped for victories in the courts were won with the help of scientists and their data. This coalition successfully got real environmental regulation through Congress and then globally.

Some scientists who came forward in the middle twentieth century also had social agendas far broader than had traditionally been the case in that profession. These hard scientists began to make common cause with sociologists and political scientists. They had similar social agendas creating real synergies in pursuit of change through political action.

However, social science is not a hard science, so facts are a bit more fluid. The political science that came into vogue in the late twentieth century took this fluidity to perverse extremes. The successes on environment issues emboldened a more socially ambiguous agenda. An anti-pollution movement joined a "return to nature" social movement, mixing their messages and politics.

In an effort to promote a less consumerist life style, scientists were rallied to prove the unsustainability of consumerism. Many predictions of disaster permeated scientific opinion in the seventies. However, much of it did not come to be true. For example, a global Ice Age was prognosticated in the seventies. Also, starvation and death due to overpopulation were forecast. Such dystopian predictions extolled a radical environmentalism wrapping issues in the context of saving the planet from humanity.

An overzealous group of social scientists and radical environmentalists overplayed the hand that scientists had used in the mid-twentieth century to advocate for necessary social change to protect the global environment. This is not to say that this overzealous group did not make tremendous progress based upon scientific data. Much of it did support their agenda. However, in their opinion society's change had not gone far enough. A more radical agenda was pushed by hyping "outlier" scientific opinions that predicted the collapse of the global ecosystem as eminent.

Fanatical environmentalism's claims in the seventies of a dark future began to erode the American public's faith in the scientific community. Time and again, dire predictions of doom came from the scientific community about overpopulation, a coming Ice Age, social collapse due to lack of food or even killer bees, all had scientific proponents. These predictions were then used to justify expensive government programs.

When the world kept rotating and social collapse did not happen, science began to look more political and less certain in its predictions. The Malthusian hysterics are what many older Americans remember from the end of the seventies. They also remember the big miss on a global Ice Age. This is what has made older generations a bit more skeptical about global warming.

Also, during this time some feel good sociological analysis of the nation's problems led to a large increase in assistance programs. The metrics being used to justify the increased social spending in welfare were based on so-called hard data. However, social science simply is not a hard science. There are many, many ways to interpret the dirty datasets of social engineers.

Their unfounded claims that there were hard metrics to support the expansive social programs began to unravel. These softer social sciences with even softer theories were used to justify expensive, yet ineffective, social programs. To Americans, they were obviously incorrect as society's ills seemed to get worse throughout the seventies.

The large and expensive failure of those same social programs was played out on the evening news. There was ever more crime on the streets in urban America according to the news media. This narrative helped substantiate some of society's growing doubts about science in general. The subsequent political fight over global climate change and what to do about it clouded facts further. In this political conflict, science begins to appear even more confused about its facts to many Americans.

Libertarian-Socialism recognizes that biology, chemistry, physics and other hard sciences allow for repeatable experimental proofs verified in controlled conditions. This is the scientific method. Theories make predictions about the real world and experiments either support those predictions or they do not.

Social sciences always have to deal with that darn unpredictable human preventing controls from being properly applied. That "data" cannot be validated to the same level of certitude. That means that repeatable experimental proofs are difficult to accomplish. The fact that experiments might have to run generations to yield results adds to uncertainty.

The push by socially concerned politicians and scientists in the late twentieth century to extract tax revenue to address societal ills backfired. The justification to American taxpayers was claimed to have been rooted in the scientific method. The reputation of American science was damaged when the promised societal improvements did not come to fruition. This is a very expensive failure, because it cost America more than dollars. The American public's belief in the objectivity of scientific fact was shattered.

Libertarian-Socialists must be aware of how we got here as a nation that now distrusts science, especially as it relates to the climate. Libertarian-Socialists must be sensitive to the twisting of the narrative about liberal scientists pushing expensive social programs morphing into a similar narrative about environmental scientists. The patriotic libertarian and the patriotic socialist understand how politics has warped all inquiry in the United States. Politics has had a hand in creating "political" science to drive social policy or agenda.

Libertarian-Socialists know that science can and will be gamed by moneyed power for political ends. With the two political parties dividing the issues, money flows to both sides of the divide. Scientists willing to write opinions for either side are on auction, so the ability to examine the quality of an argument's data matters. The duopoly has exacerbated American doubt in science by using the global climate change debate as a political football. A casualty of this is the credibility of any scientist in disagreement with the party line.

Americans continue to watch as both proponents and opponents find, or more correctly, FUND, scientific opinions and data to support their political positions. The expected consequence of so much private sponsorship of science is growing distrust of the scientific community by American citizens. Unfortunately, greedy and unethical behavior on the part of scientists has made sure that the distrust only grows.

Libertarian-Socialists understand that science has been correct about many things. However, the corruptions of American politics, corporate money and the self-righteous zeal of alleged do-gooders have caused too many scientists to lose their objectivity. Scientists have become political pawns. Libertarian-Socialists understand the scientific method. No amount of corruption by scientists changes the power of the scientific method to identify truth in the natural world for the libertarian-socialist.

The libertarian-socialist's point of view recognizes that science is done by humans and humans are flawed. Nonetheless, the scientific method remains valid and available for any that wish to use it. Here is where a grasp of the scientific method is key to differentiate between the qualities of the data in these two different types of science. Clearly, there are issues of global import that require Americans to understand what so much of the world already grasps, which is that human activity, mostly economic activity, has an effect on the global climate.

Libertarian-Socialists must help average Americans use the scientific method to sift through competing "political" science claims. This grassroots science is a tradition in the United States. America's great expansion in the industrial age was driven by the citizen scientists that sprung from practical application of technology in the real world, not academia's ivory towers. Steve Wozniak's hacking that helped create this technological world is a contemporary example of the citizen scientist.

The current distrust of science is bad for America and humanity in general. Filtering out the pollutants caused by American politics will be the great challenge. Real facts and real hard data presented through the scientific method represent the only path forward. Libertarian-Socialism can help Americans come back to the scientific side.

Climate Change Is Real, but So Are the Politics

The patriotic libertarian and the patriotic socialist have long since agreed that global climate change is real. They also agree that predictions about the ultimate outcome of the world's changing climate are speculation. This is the true hard science on the matter. The actions the world takes must be flexible due to this uncertainty. The climate is changing and at least some of that change is directly related to human activity, specifically the burning of fossil fuels. How much of the change is arguable for sure, but current temperature fluctuations are swinging beyond historical variations.

The thawing of the ancient iceboxes in the south and north of the planet are in progress. Such thawing will open a Northwest Passage to be sailed by the world's merchant sailors soon. Countries like Tuvalu in the South Pacific are struggling to keep their heads above water, literally, as sea level rise begins to shrink their flat coral atoll of a country to nothing. Venice is building a vast complex of storm doors and sea walls to protect their city from global sea level rise. The British are also spending enormous amounts of money to protect London from storm surges coming up the Thames. Oil companies are investing billions in preparation for an ice-free Arctic that will soon be open to oil drilling. Investment of these large sums of money all around the world confirm that global climate change is happening.

Another thing that is abundantly clear to patriots is that historically America has been blessed with an advantageous climate. The United States has been able to feed itself, and much of the world, via vast tracts of arable land. In fact, one of America's deepest and darkest times was related to an environmental catastrophe, the

Dust Bowl. The black blizzards of the Great Depression's Dust Bowl blighted these same vast tracts of arable land.

No one, including scientists, can be sure about how things will work out in the climate change roulette the world has begun. Perhaps things will work out in America's favor. The odds seem long that changes to the climate will preserve this inherent American advantage. The United States can hardly afford any degradation to its current climate advantage.

Weather related disasters will strain the nation's economic resources to the breaking point. Already hurricanes appear to be increasing in number due to changes in the atmosphere. These destructive storms are becoming more powerful. Tornadoes also appear to be on the increase in the breadbasket of America. Whether these trends will continue, no one can be sure, but the odds would seem to favor their continuation.

The denial of these scientific facts, which are all pointing to one conclusion, human industrial activity is affecting global climate, represents a great failure in American science. However, it is not just a failure of scientists or even of politicians. Politicians will always act like the political animals that they are and that is the one hard scientific fact about political science! Americans cannot continuously blame politicians for chasing the money as it is to be expected.

It's too easy to blame conservatives and corporations for this stunning failure to act upon the obvious. The patriotic libertarian and the patriotic socialist understand that Americans really wanted to believe these spin-doctoring scientists in the nineties. Their belief allowed them to live the lifestyle they coveted. Drilling for oil had made gasoline cheap and tooling around in a big SUV was fun.

Global climate change is often referred to as global warming. This definitely muddies things. A few excessively cold winters and skepticism grows. Over the years, both sides of the debate have taken advantage of the uncertainty of future weather predictions. Both sides have been able to field their set of scientists and experts backing a narrow point of view. It is one of the reasons why the decision to take action has been put off for so long. There seemed to be no conclusive evidence one way or another to the average American.

The patriotic conversation starts with an acceptance that human-caused climate change is a fact. However, it is also a given that there has been partisan manipulation of data on both sides. The libertarian-socialist understands global climate change is a complex issue for the average American. That complexity has been increased by politics.

Weather still defies computer models to make long-term accurate predictions. This is due to the extraordinary amount of data that needs to be processed. Scientists are still years away from achieving processing speeds that allow them to collect data and crunch the numbers in time to beat the occurrence of the weather.

Despite these shortcomings in data collection, the essential equation that is the foundation for the algorithms has been verified as sound. The Earth's weather is a large heat driven equation. As the temperature numbers being entered into the equation get bigger, one can expect bigger swings in the results.

In lay terms, this basic aspect of the equations defining weather models means one could expect colder winters, hotter summers, more and more violent hurricanes and tornadoes. Coupled with these greater more violent weather events, there will be a good deal of unexpected variability. In a nutshell, the weather will become even more unpredictable as our computer models will be unable to keep pace with the accelerating change in the real world.

Exactly how this will all play out is still beyond technology to predict with exactitude. However, that does not mean the world should take no action and simply ignore the situation. Unfortunately, politics and money have clouded the issues for decades. The doubt became so great that the debate about solutions degraded into a debate about whether it was even real. That ridiculous presumption has again reared its ugly head.

The conservative right suspects most proposed solutions to global climate change are the ravings of hippies trying to roll back America's technological society to a nature-worshiping commune. The right also claims that it wants to make policy on hard science and not on political rhetoric. Unfortunately, for the right, science supports man-made global climate change, so they must move on or be dangerous obstructionists.

Libertarian-Socialists understand that the current scientific global climate change debate is about how dramatic and how fast the global climate is changing, not whether it is changing. Additionally, the matter of global sea level rise driven by global climate change can no longer be ignored. Decades of sponsored science against human-caused climate change may have muddied the water for Americans, but now the water won't wait.

Without a doubt, there still exists reasoned debate among climate scientists globally about the ultimate outcomes. Global sea level rise is happening and accelerating as the ice caps melt. It is misguided for this reasoned debate about the extent of climate change to be seen as doubt that it is happening. IT IS HAPPENING!

The disagreement about how much sea level will ultimately rise should not be used by the naysayers on the American political right to promote ideas of no human-caused climate change happening at all. The debate is over about whether this is being caused by industrial burning of fossil fuels among other human activities. There is little doubt of human-caused climate change at this point, but years of purposeful obfuscation of the facts has become difficult to reverse.

On the other hand, there have been indications that the American environmentalist lobby has been involved in clouding issues about climate change and the solutions. The environmental left has backed their own scientific studies and been caught skewing facts on some occasions to support a political agenda. Traditional environmentalist solutions often fail to take into account some basic pragmatic realities. Many of the environmentalist sponsored climate models cannot be considered anything more than guesses due to uncertainties about the historical data and difficulty collecting real time data in the present.

In a patriotic conversation about global climate change, libertarian-socialists must make sure the debate revolves around scientific facts. Where facts are still debatable then the discussion needs to center on how to collect good data. With good data, verifiable and repeatable experiments can be used to gain more knowledge and make predictions. Predictions in the natural world are how scientific theories are tested. If the hypothesis cannot make a usable and testable prediction about the natural world, then it is subject to questioning.

Both sides are playing fast and loose with the facts. Doubts? How is it that fuel cell vehicles using hydrogen as fuel are touted as climate friendly vehicles? There is so much support that California subsidizes the purchase of a hydrogen fuel cell vehicle. However, the source of the hydrogen would most likely be coming as a byproduct of fracking in pursuit of natural gas. This seems to be a direct subsidy of extractive industry. How can this technology be touted as climate friendly?

Many will point to the relatively benign exhaust from fuel cell vehicles, which is water vapor. It is true water vapor is relatively benign, in general. However, water vapor is a greenhouse gas. There is no doubt in the scientific community that water vapor is a greenhouse gas. Water vapor is also directly related to cloud formation in normal weather, so pumping industrial amounts of water vapor into the atmosphere would seem unwise, even if water vapor was not a greenhouse gas. Water vapor is a greenhouse gas however.

How is it that so much infrastructure is being built for a hydrogen economy? How is it that large automakers have invested heavily in this technology as a climate friendly solution to personal transportation? How is it that a byproduct of fracking could be considered environmentally friendly? Is it not because they have the support of the environmental left? Libertarian-Socialists say the answer is yes.

Science supports the above statements about the climate unfriendly nature of hydrogen yet the news media, journalists, politicians and other talking heads all see fuel cell vehicles as environmentally friendly. In fact, there are plenty of scientists that will say the vehicles are environmentally friendly. Of course, there are plenty on the other side as well, but maybe not as well funded.

Hydrogen vehicles are not climate neutral. For government to subsidize the fuel cell vehicle makes no sense. The advocacy of the technology by environmental lobbyists makes even less sense. Nonetheless, there is huge support for this technology due to corruption on both sides of the political debate on climate change in this country.

Who am I? I have no formal training. I am a private citizen with an interest in science along with being a hobbyist gardener. That means I have more than a casual interest in the weather as well. Apparently, it gives me a unique point of view, because science would seem to support the contention that fuel cell vehicles are not climate friendly. Nonetheless, fuel cell vehicles are promoted as climate friendly by the "experts".

In libertarian-socialism's new paradigm, average citizens need to book up on the scientific method. Citizens need to be able to do some interpretation on their own of data relating to climate change... not to mention a whole host of other complicated issues.

Indeed this IS America. A founding father, Ben Franklin, made a prediction: Lightning is a manifestation of electricity in the natural environment, not God's vengeance. He then flew a kite on a metal string until it was struck by lightning to determine whether the model was correct. He predicted that a large electrical charge would come down the wire to the metal key he placed at the end. This is exactly what happened. He went onto invent lightning rods to protect church steeples from God's vengeance.

The citizen-scientist is part of what has made this country so amazing. Ben Franklin is an example, and there is also Thomas Edison, Robert Goddard, the Wright Brothers and even Henry Ford doing science as autodidacts. Yes, some of it is science in its most basic form, but science nonetheless. In this way, even complicated things get broken down by a legion of citizen-scientists. Consensus is created from chaos.

When experiments are not easily created and replicated, as in the case of global climate change, there is definitely room for debate. Climate science data can and has been gamed, but it still points overwhelmingly to human caused climate change. What is really being debated among responsible scientists is how much is human caused.

The other question being debated earnestly is what to do about it, but not whether it is happening. That is where libertarian-socialism will hope to energize citizen scientists. Libertarian-Socialists must help educate the people on the global climate change issue and help drive consensus on solutions. To do this, libertarian-socialism will need to take on the traditionally Democratic and liberal environmental lobbies not just the Republican and conservative lobbies.

Modular Transportation Infrastructure for the Future

The need to have a viable and consistent plan for powering the country's transportation infrastructure is obvious. The path to create such a consensus is less obvious due to financial forces obscuring the way forward. There are several competing ideas for transportation. For some, fuel cells have become the vision for the nation's transportation future. This is mostly due to moneyed power preferring this technology. The reason the hydrogen economy has gotten this far is due to these forces. Moneyed power is forcing the nation to dilute its focus by continuing to advocate for the old transportation model.

The hydrogen economy allows the fossil fuel industry to continue its business model almost unchanged into the future. It is the financial benefits bestowed upon moneyed power rather than environmental benefits that have propelled the hydrogen economy forward. Libertarian-Socialists advocate that federally sponsored renewable sources should be mandated to produce electricity. Such a political mandate provides a consistent framework for transportation infrastructure development going into the future. It also helps curtail attempts to expand the old transportation energy infrastructure.

The generation of power for the country is too important to be put in the hands of for-profit companies. The potential for profit is driving the course of energy generation in this country. Otherwise hydrogen power and fuel cell technologies would not be touted as viable solutions. When examined closely, science does not support climate-neutral claims for fuel cells and profiteering is revealed.

Individuals and corporations with a stake in building a hydrogen-based economy are behind studies that suggest hydrogen fuel cells can save the world from climate change. These fuel cells are often billed as producing nothing but innocuous water vapor. Every meteorologist knows that water vapor is a greenhouse gas and will cause climate change. Pumping industrial amounts of water vapor into the atmosphere will change the climate.

Additionally, the infrastructure that transports liquid or gas through pipelines to storage tanks to fueling stations is not the future. A hydrogen economy leverages existing infrastructure requiring its modification and expansion. This is the old model for how to fuel a nation's transportation infrastructure. The national transportation infrastructure should transition to a mostly electric model. Currently, the nation is too dependent on fossil fuels for all manner of industrial and transportation infrastructure.

The fuel cell evangelists have obvious economic motivations. Oil companies are supportive of this technology. Hydrogen can be extracted as a byproduct of fracking. That means the whole fossil fuel industry can continue its drilling and extraction. The hydrogen economy is driven by profit hungry corporations. Hydrogen does not make sense if a climate neutral energy infrastructure in the future is the goal.

Of course, the fossil fuel infrastructure should be improved and modernized as we are likely to be leaning on it for some time. However, expansion of this model for powering transportation is a dead end. It is the fossil fuel industry that wants this model to be maintained and expanded. America needs to prepare its infrastructure for the future. The future is electricity.

Settling on electricity as the energy source of the future makes sense. It allows for some modularization of the transportation infrastructure. Decoupling transportation from the source of energy generation is important. In the same way that a software application is designed in a modular fashion to allow for upgrades and changes, American transportation infrastructure needs to move toward a similar modular design. Modularity facilitates flexibility in the future.

To continue with the software application analogy, a data module will exist in the software application that abstracts the data source away from the rest of the application. A software application is most often designed so that different data sources can be accessed, because there are many out there and there will be many more in the future. This modular design for data access means if a faster or better data source comes along in the future, the application can plug-in to a different database with minimal changes. Designing our transportation infrastructure in a similar fashion makes a lot of sense.

Agreeing that the future is electricity helps push the nation's infrastructure toward this modularity. The first step to make American transportation more modular is agreeing that the goal is an electrically powered infrastructure, not a chemical fuel based one. Modularity means as the United States builds out alternative energy production, the current dirty fossil fuel back end generation can be swapped out.

The United States will be able to plug in any and all electrical generation sources to its transportation infrastructure. As other alternatives come online and become more viable, the transportation infrastructure will already be electrified and ready to plug in to the new source. The future will not have to evolve a completely new transportation infrastructure as energy generation capabilities evolve. America will just plug in the new electrical generation sources and the infrastructure just keeps humming along.

Electrical generation and easy transportation of that energy all over the national grid is a requirement for the future. Concentrating on building out, enhancing and expanding the nation's electrical infrastructure is an absolute necessity. Instead of diluting efforts between chemically-powered transportation and electrical-powered transportation, a more robust electrical infrastructure should be built out.

An additional benefit of a modular transportation infrastructure bathed in electricity is that more electricity-dependent vehicles can be put on the roads as well. Current hybrid technologies involve lots of exotic metals for the batteries used to store the electrical energy like a gas tank. This is making current hybrid automaker's green claims somewhat suspect.

A better solution would be a different kind of hybrid. These hybrids would have gasoline engines for around town but electric motors that could be powered on the interstates. This is an important part of the build out of a national transportation infrastructure that is based upon electricity. Small internal combustion engines coupled with electric motors are far more environmentally friendly vehicles due to the reduction in need for batteries and exotic metals. The electric motors will be powered in the "electric lane" of national interstates via wireless power transmission or direct connections embedded in the road rather than carrying batteries.

This different hybrid model eliminates the pollution-intensive batteries from the equation. This model allows an electric car to have a much larger range over an electrified interstate system. Small gasoline powered hybrids in town with the ability to couple to an electrified interstate system allows for the best of both worlds. It also allows for a gradual transition away from fossil fuels as more local infrastructure is built out.

The world needs immediate solutions more than ever. We as a nation need to have a clear and consistent plan into the future. Wasting our precious financial resources on things like building out a hydrogen fueled transportation infrastructure is dangerous folly. Such financial expenditures are more about lining the pockets of opportunistic profiteers with government connections, than actually building a new and practical energy generation infrastructure.

Fission or Frickin' Fracking

Lack of pragmatic reform from environmental activists has painted the United States, no check that, the world, into a corner. America continued burning cheap oil all throughout the last decade of the twentieth century. Oil was so cheap nothing could compete on price. Americans have opposed a tax on a gallon of gas ever since independent presidential candidate John Anderson proposed it in his 1980 campaign. Americans WANT cheap oil!

In America, it is easy to talk about saving the environment, but if it makes gas prices go up, then nobody can stomach it. Many environmentalists preach conservation. Through conservation, they say, the United States can reduce emissions. Throughout most of its history, the environmental establishment has focused on what industry and people cannot do rather than what they can do. This has made Americans look at environmentalists as job killers and impractical dreamers.

The idea of a pro-nuclear environmentalist is an oxymoron to many. The events in Japan at Fukushima seem to have killed nuclear power as an energy option…again…just as Chernobyl and Three Mile Island did back in the eighties. However, the climate has deteriorated significantly during this time, so perhaps the world is ready to reconsider fission, warts and all. Global climate change has reached a tipping point. Ignoring atomic fission is no longer tenable when one considers all the facts, even in light of Fukushima. Nuclear power is the last hope of maintaining a high standard of living in conjunction with a relatively clean environment.

The libertarian-socialist must step forward to give the public the whole story concerning nuclear power. The ideologically motivated claptrap that has been used to persuade the American public to drop nuclear power as an energy source is criminal in its misrepresentation of the facts. A future without nuclear power can only be a grim one for this planet, but especially for the United States of America. The Earth's climate stability cannot stand another generation of fossil fuel combustion, like the last.

We now know that the major oil companies knew climate change was happening back in the eighties. Congruently, there was a global anti-nuclear weapons movement that was gaining enormous transaction. It became widely understood that nuclear weapons were doomsday devices. It did not take but a fraction of the mega-tonnage available to trigger a nuclear winter. The anti-nuclear weapons movement began to target nuclear reactors as well. It was a bit off base, since weapons were not being made at the facilities, but the "No Nukes" movement encompassed all things nuclear.

Oil companies were preparing to drill in an ice free Arctic even in the eighties. One wonders what other forward thinking plans these companies implemented. In retrospect, one wonders how much oil companies spent to manipulate the fledgling "No Nukes" movement. It probably did not take too much money at all to point them at their main competitors for electrical production. The nineties were a decade with some of the cheapest oil, relatively, that had been seen in many people's lifetimes. This seriously crippled alternative energy sources. Fission needed a more concerted effort to cripple its development and "No Nukes" provided that.

Some have pointed to Chernobyl as the real cause of fission's decline. Certainly a case can be made. The accident had a hand in hastening the end for the Soviet Union no doubt. That nation's reputation was deeply damaged by the nuclear accident. This can be partly attributed to the Russians lying about the state of affairs at the reactor. Their lies were transparent to the world's Geiger counters and destroyed many trusting national relationships.

Fukushima and the radioactivity fears that nuclear energy drags around like a boat anchor are overblown. These fears have a real basis in fact of course. Radioactivity is invisible and dangerous. However, one of the beautiful things about nuclear power and radioactivity is that Geiger counters are cheap. It is extremely difficult, if not impossible to hide nuclear reactor problems, like radioactivity leaks.

Unlike other technologies and chemicals like the MTBE groundwater pollution that cleaned up California's air only to destroy large portions of the state's water supplies, radiation leaks are very easy for the public to detect with inexpensive Geiger counters. At Fukushima, like Chernobyl, it is impossible for governments and corporations to cover up what is going on and how bad things really are. The patriotic libertarian and the patriotic socialist understand that ease of detection is a huge positive for nuclear fission.

Fukushima is a near worst-case scenario in Japan, a 9.0 earthquake and an 80-foot tsunami hit the reactors. Yet the world did not see the kind of enormous radiation leaks such as what was released at Chernobyl. Also worthy of consideration is that Fukushima is a very old design from decades ago. If this level of safety from an obsolete architecture does not give people some confidence, it is hard to imagine what will.

Libertarian-Socialists understand that energy production is a national security issue as great as any other. The United States is heavily involved in the wars and unrest in oil producing regions due to its dependence on foreign oil. Nuclear fission is the lesser of two evils, but certainly the lesser. Precisely because it is not perfect, means that environmentalists must get involved in the production of energy by fission.

Libertarian-Socialists will advocate the government nationalization of all nuclear generating facilities to be operated as national public utilities. The lessons of Enron's manipulation of energy generation to boost profits demonstrates the need to nationalize. Libertarian-Socialists also believe that involving environmentalists as watchdogs of nationalization is a necessary action to get "buy-in" from this active segment.

Environmentalists must accept the need for nuclear fission and buy in to an agenda for its development. Environmentalists have a role, as government watchdogs, to make sure the bureaucrats do not cut corners at the expense of the environment and safety. Fission is really the only option for always available industrial amounts of power, but we all understand it is not perfect.

Just as many alternative energy sources are imperfect. There is no silver bullet. Alternate energy sources are subject to the vagaries of weather and still have a ways to go before they can replace current electrical generation methods. The generation of industrial amounts of electrical power on demand is a tall order. Excess electricity generated on especially sunny or windy days cannot be stored.

Germany, which moved away from fission in favor of renewables, has actually increased its carbon emissions. This is in conjunction with setting records for renewable power generation. Unfortunately, when there is no wind or sun, then electricity must be generated by oil or natural gas or COAL! Solar, tidal, wind and geo-thermal technologies are worth pursuing, but pouring the lion share of our precious financial resources into these technologies is not practical.

Huge amounts of electricity will be required for a transition to an electric transportation infrastructure. Some studies have shown that a plug-in all electric car will actually generate more carbon emissions. Using current power generation technologies an electric car may actually produce more pollution than the current internal combustion car does.

This is because the energy has to be created offsite and then transported to the vehicle. Creation of the power within the vehicle by burning gasoline is far more efficient. Because less energy is used to travel a given distance in a gasoline automobile, less pollution is created. This is not talked about enough.

The amount of money that the United States has dumped into the Middle East to preserve access to oil and energy is truly appalling. The only reason why this has been done is that there has been no other alternative in the minds of the leaders of this country. The lack of ideas has convinced the citizenry that there is no other path but occupying the oil fields. However, given the amount of money evaporated by Middle East military actions, a case could be made that some of that money might be better spent securing the energy grid here at home and powering it up to its maximum.

Fission is a proven industrial strength energy generator. Nuclear energy does not suffer from the limitations of weather nor does it produce significant climate changing emissions. Another factor rarely considered by those advocating alternative energy generation plants is how much the climate has already changed and is changing. We must spend billions to blanket an area of desert with solar panels or put wind turbines in the Great Plains. What if that desert becomes overcast due to climate change or tornadoes increase enormously and start tearing up the wind farm? Environmentalists have no answer.

Libertarian-Socialists can hear the environmental apologists now. Who knew a hurricane would hit California? Uh, anybody paying attention to the weather ought to know that the storm track feeding storms into Mexico is gradually shifting north. Typhoons, Pacific hurricanes, are already sending remnants into the Golden State. It would only take a slight left turn in Baja for a typhoon to come roaring out of the Gulf of California potentially destroying any solar energy electric generation plant in the Mojave. We cannot spend money on these huge projects without understanding how the weather is going to evolve and we just don't know that.

Environmentalists must understand unless the electricity is generated without atmospheric emissions, an electrical transportation infrastructure, can solve nothing. Nuclear fission can provide the juice. Atomic reactors can bring about a practical future based on fission-generated electricity. The United States will get additional synergies as well from a clear and focused build out of nuclear generated electricity generation.

No matter how things evolve in the future, it starts with embracing fission technology as it stands. The world and America in particular cannot survive another twenty years of fossil fuel combustion like the previous twenty or even the previous ten years. Time is short to mitigate loss of America's climate advantages. The reality is that it is fission or frickin' fracking…that is the real choice.

Radioactive Waste Conundrum

A strong objection to nuclear power is that nuclear waste disposal techniques are inadequate. The fact that waste created by reactors is toxic for centuries is certainly a persuasive argument against a fission-powered electrical grid. What exactly to do with the radioactive waste seems to be an insoluble conundrum. However, when other power sources are held to the same standard, it becomes a shared problem.

Current disposal methods for spent fossil fuels are non-existent. The world does not trap the exhaust from fossil fuel combustion and put it into barrels. Instead, the global population spews the poisonous byproducts into the atmosphere. The waste products of fission are put into barrels and its whereabouts cataloged. Admittedly, those barrels will be hazardous for many thousands of years. In contrast, the waste products of fossil fuels hang around to affect the environment and weather detrimentally for an unknown period.

The analogy of an urban sewer system is useful when considering the nuclear power situation. The lack of adequate fossil fuel waste disposal condemns the world to breathe its own excrement. With nuclear fission, humanity can at least put its waste into a septic tank. A comparison of waste disposal techniques would seem to indicate that fossil fuels are far more toxic due to the difficulty in containing the waste. What is the half-life of fossil fuel waste asks the libertarian-socialist?

Finding a place to store those barrels of radioactive waste has been a great problem. However, given that there are large expanses of desert in the American West contaminated by years of nuclear testing, why not use these areas for storing barrels of nuclear waste.

The American government set off hundreds of nuclear bombs a mere sixty-five miles from Las Vegas in the fifties and sixties. Over one hundred of these atomic bomb tests were above ground. The blasts were visible for miles around. Stacking some barrels of spent nuclear fuel there seems trivial in comparison.

The NIMBY effect has dogged America's quest for energy independence. Americans need to consider heavy subsidies to any state storing radioactive waste. There are some clear candidates for being the store house states, though. Libertarian-Socialists would encourage Americans to compensate those candidates and for those candidates to be patriotic. The generation of energy is a national security issue. If ever the need for eminent domain had a justification, this could be it.

Libertarian-Socialists know the American public has an overwhelming fear of nuclear reactors. Three Mile Island scared many people. The amount of radiation released at Three Mile Island should be put into perspective, though. A declassified document from the nineties revealed details of a nuclear experiment that went awry, code named Green Run. In the late fifties, near Spokane, Washington, nearly eight thousand curies of radiation were released. By contrast, the Three Mile Island incident released barely forty curies. Forty curies are not good, but in comparison to what occurred over fifty years ago, it is minor.

The Green Run experimental failure could no longer even occur nowadays, because the world has too many Geiger counters. Back then nobody had a Geiger counter so the secret could be kept. Clearly, radioactivity was still treated too cavalierly. The government was actually doing open air burst bomb tests for decades after WWII. There is one powerful lesson from this careless radioactive pollution that occurred, however. The fallout from this carelessness seems to have been dissipated by natural processes.

The Green Run experiment and the legacy of air burst atomic bomb testing in the Nevada desert are illustrative of the fact that radiation is a natural aspect of the environment. It is just as subject to natural processes as the waste of fossil fuels and perhaps more so. Thousands, perhaps millions, of curies of radiation were released into the air during the Green Run fiasco and other secret tests.

However, the government was able to conceal its errors only due to the widespread lack of Geiger counters at the time. This is terrible, of course, but imagine trying to cover up a similar fossil fuel error.

Obviously, the environment has some capacity to dissipate radiation. Uranium is a natural ore, and many areas on Earth are naturally radioactive to some extent. An oil slick, thousands of square miles wide, could never be swept under the rug by the government. If no clean up action is taken such an oil slick could destroy an environment for decades, perhaps centuries. The environment does not seem to dissipate fossil fuel pollution all that easily. Before the days of cheap Geiger counters, hiding radiation leaks was not that hard, but the damage from huge oil spills has always been clear for all to see.

The environment does not effectively assimilate oil. Even though the Gulf of Mexico now appears relatively clean, the millions of barrels of oil spilled by Deepwater Horizon still lurk about in the water damaging the health of its inhabitants. In Prince William Sound, the Exxon Valdez accident was far worse than Three Mile Island. It was painful to watch the footage coming from Alaska's Prince William Sound. The animal suffering was so great, even more so than appeared to be the case in the Gulf of Mexico. News footage of workers wiping off Alaska's rocky beaches with towels would have been laughable, had it not been so tragic.

The world runs on oil. War after war in the Middle East has horribly fouled the Persian Gulf. Arabian marine life will never be the same. Chernobyl, arguably the worst nuclear reactor accident, has left a legacy of nature reserves. Truly, the lack of humanity in the Chernobyl "dead zone" has produced a wealth of wildlife and regeneration of the ecology none would have predicted. One has to doubt that a similar nature reserve is being created in the Gulf of Mexico in the aftermath of Deep Water Horizon's oil spill.

These petroleum disasters will only recur. Tankers and pipelines crisscross the globe. Thousands of potential disasters are waiting to happen every day. In fact, these accidents are happening, but Geiger counters do not pick up oil spills. Major spills are hard to cover up, but continuous minor spillage here and there takes its toll silently with no Geiger counter to sniff it out. The risks of petroleum actually seem greater when compared to the risks of fission, since radioactive waste cannot be hidden.

For some reason there is little discussion of how radioactive waste can be further reduced by a simple action. The government currently allows civilian reactors to use only low-grade nuclear fuel. This is due to national security concerns. Low-grade fuel creates far more waste than necessary. Nationalization of fission should ease national security concerns, so that these reactors can be run on purer fuel. Such spent nuclear fuel can be used in breeder reactors further to reduce waste, not something that can be done in the case of fossil fuels.

Nationalization would allow the reactors to burn high grade, ninety-nine percent pure fuel, as the military does. This would decrease the amount of waste created significantly. Breeder reactors can use this spent fuel more efficiently as well to reduce the waste produced even further. There is no question that radioactive waste produced by fission is a difficult problem, but it is not insoluble. In addition, when radioactive waste handling is compared to the handling of fossil fuel waste, the latter process seems almost criminal in its inadequacy.

Ironically, it might also ease some concern to know that radioactive waste is being produced in a whole host of different arenas. There is quite a bit of radioactive waste produced in the medical arena and no one thinks that nuclear medicine should be banned. Americans need to understand that fracking and other extractive efforts produce an enormous amount of radioactive waste. If Americans knew, would fracking even be tolerated?

Water for Drinking, Irrigation and Terraforming

Energy scarcity warps society in so many ways, but the crisis that a water shortage could bring is exponentially worse. For all the aforementioned reasons, nuclear power is a good idea. However, there is another reason that Americans should embrace fission. Its implementation brings a lot more juice into the electrical grid. The United States can use that extra electricity to help bring a solution to its growing water problems.

Any doubts Americans have about the state of water quality in America should be dispelled by the statistics on how much bottled water Americans are drinking. Only those that cannot afford anything else, drink tap water regularly in America. Those individuals, like the people of Flint, Michigan, may be sacrificing their health by doing so. Americans pay taxes for water treatment and safe drinking water, but most Americans do not believe that tap water is safe.

The horrible water treatment scandal in Flint has brought the issue of drinking water to the forefront of the nation's consciousness for the first time since the Tennessee Valley Authority. The TVA electrified rural America and stopped the periodic flooding that plagued the region stabilizing drinking water supplies. Scientific analysis of water quality in America certainly confirms the existence of drug residues in water samples all across America. The American government has admitted that America's water supply contains trace amounts of many polysyllabic chemicals and drugs.

As bad as the current situation is the future may be much worse. Minor pollutants in the water may not matter in the future, because just having water that is treatable will be a problem. Global climate change is playing havoc with the twentieth century water distribution networks of dams and aqueducts, such as the TVA.

Dams in the West, no longer work as designed, due to the early snow melts that are now occurring. Even in years where the Sierra and Rockies get the expected amounts of snow pack, early spring rains and warming melts the snow pack much faster than in the past. Water that will be needed in the warm summer months has to be released because the dam fills too soon. Not only that, the West's many hydroelectric dams produce much less power under these climate conditions. That means there is even greater need for fission to make up the difference without spewing more pollutants into the air.

Instead of a slower melt that allows spring usage to draw down the reservoir to make room for subsequent late spring melting, the fast melts mean the dam fills too fast and cannot be drawn down over time. Additional snow melt ends up in the ocean, because there is no room. Then in the summer, reservoirs are lower than they otherwise would have been. That can mean there is no late spring melt water to quench the summer and autumn thirst. Or water to release from hydroelectric dams to power air conditioners in the hot summer months.

As the patriotic libertarian and the patriotic socialist discuss the nation's issues, the crisis in water quality and availability sneaks its way up the priority list as the facts are surfaced. Widespread water shortages seem almost a certainty sometime in the future. It really depends upon when a long enough drought hits a large region of the nation. Droughts are coming more often and are getting longer in the West. One can conclude that eventually the current infrastructure will be overwhelmed.

There is only one way to deal with this situation and that is to build desalinization plants. How many the United States will need depends on how much climate changes affect the American continent's rainfall patterns. Desalinization plants are very expensive in dollars and energy terms. It takes an enormous amount of energy to desalinate seawater. Nuclear power will allow the country to have the necessary energy to run these desalinization plants at some kind of reasonable price.

Desalinization has become the only answer. Not only has global climate change affected America's water supplies, there has been foolish destruction of the nation's own fresh water supplies. Fresh water has been lost due to the pollution of groundwater by dependence on polysyllabic chemicals and fossil fuels. MTBEs have destroyed groundwater supplies all over California. These chemicals were meant to help gasoline burn cleaner and, therefore, reduce air pollution. Air pollution has been reduced, but at the expense of groundwater, a fool's bargain.

Fracking being used to extract natural gas might reduce air pollution as well, but the groundwater risks created by fracking are enormous. Enormous amounts of chemically treated water injected into cracks in the bedrock cannot be controlled despite industry promises to the contrary. Discussions of how the waste water is controlled are fantasies at best.

The fracking risk to the groundwater supply would seem to rule it out as a normal common practice, but it has powerful lobbyists in its favor. The oil drilling and exploration companies certainly are among them. It allows them to continue their business model unchanged into a warmer future.

America's abundant water allows for irrigation of enormous tracts of arable lands. Water is one of America's great blessings. The United States has squandered the resource and may never enjoy the same abundance due to climate change and negligence. America needs climate change to be mitigated, because one of the pillars of the nation's greatness is a favorable climate. Desalinization plants will allow continued irrigation of farmlands, as climate change could severely reduce American rainfall totals.

Given the long-term advantages that climate has provided America in geopolitics, preventing large-scale climate change is strongly in the national interest. There are some ways, all of them expensive, to handle this environmental crisis. Controlling the climate is beyond American scientific abilities, but the nation can seek to ally itself with those that have been the great climate moderators of history: plant life. Plants and trees filter the atmosphere and transform it by producing oxygen from carbon dioxide and water. They can help tamp down the urban heat islands that have been created within cities as well.

A large program dedicated to the replanting of native species in the many different microclimates that make up the nation can help stabilize the continent's climate. Because normal rainfall patterns will likely be changing, the United States may need to irrigate new native stands of trees. It will take decades for the trees to have a positive effect on climate. These huge stands of native plant life will also act as a buffer to pollution that the Asian continent will surely be sending east as these economies continue to expand exponentially. Desalinization plants can facilitate irrigation of large areas that the nation must return to its native flora to mitigate climatological disaster.

Additionally, there is a growing salinity problem in the nation's soil. Irrigation, repeated fertilizer use, and population growth have put enormous pressure on the fertile, rich western farmlands. The earliest civilizations in Mesopotamia were based on irrigated farmlands. It was the salinity in their soils that ended the civilizations of the Fertile Crescent after centuries of prosperity. The world now knows these fertile lands to be desertified Iraq.

Desalinization plants will help flush the salt out of soils over time. It will cost billions to pull it off, but it will gradually pay dividends and, in the end, preserve America's climate advantage. With so much money necessary to pull this off, citizens will need to be heavily involved to give politicians the will to spend the money and make an investment that will not have any short-term benefits.

There will be huge dividends over the long run, though. Libertarian-Socialists embrace this as a common sense plan even though it sounds quite speculative. The use of tax dollars in support of public utilities allows for taking the long view. This is what a libertarian-socialist Green New Deal looks like.

Adopting these policies will not only preserve America's climate advantage, but will also act as stimulus. Simultaneous institution of such a comprehensive energy production/climate change initiative will create jobs galore. Such sector stimulus packages have historically created jobs. There is every reason to believe they will do so again. The state of the national treasury mandates that government money spent from now on, not only creates jobs, but also builds out an infrastructure to serve the nation into the future. This libertarian-socialist plan for the nation's drinking water does exactly that!

Social Support with a New Currency

The concept of a universal income credit is a familiar one today. In a nutshell, the government guarantees a minimum income for all of its citizens. Certainly from the socialist point of view as well as the consumerist one, this is something that makes a lot of sense. Capitalists obviously need convincing, but even these hardcore purists are considering ideas like universal basic income. In the eyes of even capitalists, the universal income subsidy seems necessary to prevent the ending of the consumer paradise that America has been.

The libertarian-socialist is a different political animal though. Libertarian-Socialists cast a suspicious eye on direct subsidies from the government and economic activity that has no point. In the patriotic conversation between the libertarian and the socialist, there is a baseline agreement always to consider direct government subsidies as a last resort.

Libertarian-Socialists accept that the central government has a role in a nation's life. It is understood that the power of the central government lies in its ability to make policy. Policies that can provide revenue can also have dramatic and unexpected effects on the society. The tax laws and programs that are instituted amount to social engineering. The libertarian-socialist understands this clearly. Therefore such policies should be used sparingly and thoughtfully. Legislation coming from the central government has enormous power to shape commerce and culture.

The consequences of tax laws and programs have become better understood with more than a century of active social engineering coming from Washington, DC. Some of that engineering was good and some of it bad. Unfortunately, the better understanding of consequences has not necessarily made for better policy. The laws and programs can be gamed for profit and understanding tends to get leveraged there.

Real estate brokers have been playing this game for decades as they see a direct benefit to sitting on a city council where zoning laws affect property values. This is just small potatoes compared to what federal tax law can do to assets. The proper positioning before a large change in the law brings revenue streams to legislators and corporations, but perhaps not the people. This has been occurring for too long at a national level in the United States.

Nonetheless, sometimes subsidies from the central government are necessary. They are a dangerous solution though. Subsidies from the central government are the most corrupting and most destructive when they are in the form of raw payments. Libertarian-Socialists understand there can be nothing more demotivating than giving money for doing nothing. As government subsidies become revenue streams, they can reduce workforce participation and the innovation that participation brings.

This is a primary reason for libertarian-socialists to oppose the universal basic income. The corrupting influences on people and politicians are just too great. Most politicians have a different understanding about giving money, so they may go forward with it. If one's goal is to be reelected, supplying bread and circuses to the citizenry is a tried and true method to retain popularity. Roman emperors used it for centuries to stay in power.

Due to their very nature, politicians cannot find the correct path for the populace as a whole even when they are looking. The fog of money always obscures the way. It falls to the citizenry to find and choose the correct path. Only then can the politicians be enlightened and be pressured to execute the path forward illuminated by the people.

Supreme Court rulings treating corporations as citizens are an expected consequence of so much money flooding the entire system. Large and powerful entities are now operating in the public space as if they were individual citizens lobbying their representatives. This corporate occupation of the legislative agenda has squeezed all, but the most powerful individuals from the public discourse. Government's admirable concern about maintaining a growing pool of jobs for citizens has been subverted by corporations. Corporations now enjoy favorable treatment as some kind of super-citizen as long as they promise that they will supply jobs to regular citizens.

Lately, "jobs" in legislative bills has been increasingly defined by the amount of profit a given industry or corporation will make. This leads to a corruption of the process, because the profit does not always trickle down. Without a doubt, corporations need customers for profits and customers need jobs to have money to buy corporate products. However, just making sure an industry is profitable does not necessarily lead to jobs.

This implied connection has led to policies vetted by profit-making potential and not by what is best for the citizenry over the long run. The role of government then begins to morph into that of a shepherd rather than a real manifestation of a nation's collective hopes and desires. A shepherd government acts to maintain a healthy working populace, which it herds toward corporate barns where the populace are milked.

This is the line of thinking that might get the universal basic income implemented in the United States. The patriotic libertarian has convinced the patriotic socialist that an ownership society is a goal. Ownership breeds independent citizens, but not necessarily good consumers. Creating good consumers will be the reason the political right comes to embrace the universal basic income.

Libertarian-Socialists believe this would only accelerate the shepherd role that the government has taken on, however. The maintenance of a healthy populace is tied to a certain income level that provides for the consumer society to continue unchanged. The revenues for such a government program would have to come from taxes and most likely from corporate taxes. This will heighten the feedback loop between corporate profits and consumer dollars that creates a citizenry that is more a herd to be managed than a living and breathing nation of people.

A libertarian-socialist has a different vision, a synergy between government and citizenry. The libertarian-socialist postulates a currency besides money that could come from the central government.

There is currently a breakdown in the social contract between the central government and the citizenry. Libertarian-Socialism seeks an innovative way for the society to support its citizenry in a fundamentally different way than a direct subsidy. The kind of citizen support that reboots the social contract. Libertarian-Socialism imagines something that encourages work rather than doing nothing for an income subsidy.

Libertarian-Socialism has driven home the need for fission energy in the United States. Fission reactors can provide a world where electricity is being generated in surplus. This world is possible if the nation decides that energy production is truly a national security issue. A national security issue that needs to be taken away from the private market.

There are too many real world and recent examples of deregulated energy markets leading to chaos. Enron's gaming of California's deregulated energy market at the turn of this century is a compelling example of how deregulation led directly to fraud and criminal behavior. Nationalizing energy production makes sense on so many different levels. This is just another one.

Nationalization can drive overproduction of electricity for the benefit of all. Imagine a surplus of energy within the United States created by a full embrace of electricity generated by atomic fission. It would now be within the power of the central government to subsidize energy, specifically electricity, which tangentially subsidizes a new electrical-first transportation.

Now the basis for a new "currency" exists and that is electricity. Electricity can be used to fund an alternative to universal basic income. A universal energy credit would mean that a citizen would be entitled to a certain amount of electricity. Ideally, enough of a surplus can be created that eventually a citizen would be entitled to as much electricity as they can put to good use. However, in the beginning it would be some large fraction of their usage.

By supplying the energy to the citizen rather than the money, the society encourages work, but still supports the citizenry. In the case of free electricity, having a roof over one's head and a computer or other equipment can lead to an income based upon work rather than simply existing. This is important to the society as a whole, but to the individual even more. The universal basic income makes a good portion of the society completely dependent on the central government to supply them with their livelihood. This is not a healthy relationship between the citizens and the central government.

The universal energy credit helps people create their own income. The universal energy credit creates independent citizens rather than dependents. Dependent citizens become a voting constituency whose focus is preserving their income stream. Preservation of their revenue stream may or may not be in the best interest of the nation as a whole. A nation that encourages its citizens to be independent, creative and innovative creates a constituency that helps lead and that helps build the country.

Talk of peak oil has been tossed about for a long time and yet it seems that there is always enough oil to burn. Moreover, if ever the world ran out of oil, the burning of coal is the current default backup today. In fact, there is more coal than the world knows what to do with. There are nuclear and renewable sources to be considered as well.

A case can be made that there is enough energy in the world and scarcity is actually created by the market makers. In addition, if one looks at geopolitics over the last century, it is the pursuit of energy or the protection of access that has driven a lot of strife. Again, energy production is clearly a national security issue. Given the amount of military effort that is required to maintain access to these energy resources, it is not that free of a market actually.

In fact, the energy market is heavily subsidized by the military efforts of this nation. In light of that, the case for nationalizing energy production in the United States is even stronger. Energy production is a national security issue. That is why this nation supports an enormous military effort to maintain the global fossil fuel network. The nation is currently dependent on it for survival.

A nationalized energy grid can provide energy to the whole United States. The nationalized energy grid can be leveraged by individuals who create their own incomes. This leveraging leads to economic expansion. Moving forward, subsidizing energy will be a very gradual iterative process. A gradual nationalization of energy production allows for continuous auditing of the costs of the production of energy. Energy production within the United States will become a not for profit industry in this model.

The universal energy credit's positive effect is multiplied by energy production being nationalized to facilitate the goal. The universal energy credit's ability to create new dynamics and nurture the meritocracy is limited if energy production is not nationalized. Simple subsidies to energy bills will be absorbed by private industry without nationalization. With a nationalized energy grid, the people can operate this vital national security asset in the interests of the greater good rather than for profit. Libertarian-Socialists recognize this is social engineering. However, it is the twenty-first century and new ideas are exactly what the United States needs.

As energy production becomes nationalized and is operated not for profit, individuals paying a hypothetical average of one hundred dollars a month for electricity can now put that money to other uses. Such a subsidy is a method to support the consumer society most Americans want. It is also a way to create the rising tide that can lift all of the boats directly, the way a tide should.

A universal basic income can never be sufficient despite being essential to many a socialist Utopian vision. The consumerist vision has now begun to embrace the universal basic income as well. Libertarian-Socialists believe there would be many corrupting effects on society were the United States to give money to people because they got up that morning. A universal energy subsidy requires some effort for the receiver to maximize the positive effect it can have on their life.

The universal energy credit is the kind of carrot that creates American social structures that help people achieve success. This is what a real Green New Deal looks like. The United States spends too much time creating sticks to drive people this way or that. The fact is the United States government's role is not to drive its citizens like sheep to corporate barns where they can be sheared. A universal basic income turns citizens of the United States into livestock. The universal energy subsidy treats United States citizens like creative individuals capable of extraordinary things given adequate support from their nation.

A successful implementation of the universal energy credit

would give libertarian-socialists the ammunition to take on an even more powerful monopoly hindering American citizens. In the case of electricity production there is at least a history of operation as a public utility in the national interest. The next target to be operated in the national interest should be high speed internet access. The technology companies have mountains of cash to oppose such an initiative. However, in the same way that free access to a national transportation infrastructure facilitated commerce within twentieth century America, free access to a national information infrastructure would do the same for twenty-first century America. The opposition to such a nationalization will be vehement, but a successful implementation of the libertarian-socialist Green New Deal will be a powerful example of what Americans can do when freed from the shackles of monopoly.

Obstacles to Success

Not to recognize the institutional and cultural obstacles to implementation of the libertarian-socialist agenda is foolish. Libertarian-Socialists are not fools. Their discussions are filled with passion, but not foolish partisan attacks. The passion for their ideas is fueled by their patriotism. The patriotic libertarian and the patriotic socialist are able to have a civil discussion due to their deeply held belief that each is a patriot. That patriotism coupled with a clear recognition that this nation is in trouble means they earnestly seek solutions.

Libertarian-Socialists will be faced by other real patriots that will oppose this agenda due to their strict adherence to a certain political dogma. This dogma has a powerful hold on people due to an "ideological fervor" created by moneyed power usurping media outlets and the levers of government. This book would not be complete without writing about these formidable obstacles to libertarian-socialism. These obstacles are very real. Ideological dogma has a tight grip upon those on each side of the left/right schism.

The passionate discussions that only a patriotic American socialist and a patriotic American libertarian can have are fiery. In the end, this book is distilled down to what the patriotic libertarian and the patriotic socialist could agree upon as solutions. This nation is wracked by problems, so solutions that can be agreed upon are vital.

The nation is on the edge of serious social unrest. The following obstacles are volatile issues. Getting broad agreement upon the way forward will be difficult. The libertarian-socialist must speak softly here, yet wield the big stick of rational patriotism when necessary.

The Unsustainable Cost of Continuous Global Conflict

The patriotic libertarian and the patriotic socialist recognize the damage that wartime profiteers have done to this nation. The military-industrial complex has been a boom sector in twenty-first century America. Despite President Dwight Eisenhower's expressed warnings always to be suspicious of the military-industrial complex, the United States is spending an enormous amount of money on the military.

General Eisenhower was the man that led America to victory in World War II and his opinion on military matters held in high regard. The political power of the defense industry is a shocking state of affairs given his clear and unambiguous warning upon turning over the reins of power to John F. Kennedy. They were strong words that General Eisenhower used in his farewell address, words like, "… conscious or unconscious manipulations of policy."

Eisenhower understood that given the potential windfall that wartime profiteering could bring to business, many business leaders cannot help but be overly prejudiced toward military action. As president, Eisenhower ended active combat operations in Korea and refused to take military action against the Soviets in Eastern Europe. He also stifled military involvement in Vietnam.

The last president who was also a general felt a lot of pressure from civilians to use the military during his term, but multiple times, he resisted. However, the pressure was apparently so great that he practically called the defense industry unpatriotic and advised the American people to mistrust perpetually the military-industrial complex as he exited office.

Eisenhower believed the United States was founded to be a

nation of civilians. More than once, the general commented on how many elementary schools could be built for the cost of ONE long-range bomber. In his vision, civilian society was supposed to lead and restrain the military. War was necessary, but peace was to be embraced and nurtured. Peace was a time for infrastructure and people investment. A concept he felt he should emphasize on his exit.

When the general who won World War II spoke, one would expect Americans to listen, but the pressure to act forcefully in national confrontation is hard to resist. Playground posturing and real fear make it hard to resist reaching for the weaponry, especially when the United States has so much at its disposal. Couple these issues with the possibility of large profits on small skirmishes against under armed opponents along with the temptations of greed and it leads to a very one-sided debate in favor of deploying military resources.

Without a persistent vigilance and energy from the citizenry, the military-industrial complex has become more powerful legislatively. Every confrontation has the potential to yield billions in profit for those that supply the necessary goods of war. With corporate concentrations in the media, it is far too easy to fill the news cycle with vitriol. With the drive for profits underlying everything, sponsored infotainment has no viable way to communicate global confrontation in anything close to an objective fashion. A very, very dangerous groupthink has set in sans any unscrupulous intentions. It is what Ike means when he refers to "...conscious or <u>unconscious</u> manipulations."

Many large corporations in America are making money from military contracts today and most of the rest have revenue streams tangentially tied to the defense industry whether they are aware or not. That simple fact energizes defense industry lobbyists, because so many American jobs are also tied to these industries. These lobbyists are driving the debate in Washington, DC. The United States has spent almost two decades of active war and foreign occupation to start this century with no end in sight and no specific accomplishments to cite as progress.

This situation cannot continue. The costs of endless global deployments is unimaginable, which is why the Pentagon has never stood for an audit. Most likely, the Department of Defense could not pass such a review without trillions being unaccounted for in the end. On September 10, 2001, Secretary of Defense Donald Rumsfeld admitted that almost two trillion was unaccounted for from previous DOD budgets. This was before any of the twenty-first century military deployments, so one can hardly be optimistic about the current state of the DOD budget. In 2016, the Office of the Inspector General (OIG) issued a report which indicated for fiscal year 2015 the Army failed to provide adequate support for $6.5 trillion in journal voucher adjustments on a $120 billion budget!

The United States is spending billions every day. As part of these military deployments, the country is also incurring future financial obligations of incalculable proportions with almost no debate. These future obligations are rarely discussed as part of the debate on defense spending, but they are very real and essentially unfunded. It is a dirty business this "Global War on Terror." Meeting recruiting goals in such a murky and dangerous enterprise is not that easy. There are enlistment bonuses amounting to tens of thousands of dollars and "stop loss" incentives to get soldiers to reenlist, which are large future obligations to veterans and their families.

Many civilians are probably unaware that the military has been offering greater and greater incentives for enlistees and even more for those that reenlist. These incentives are not small and extend beyond the soldier to subsequent generations. These incentives essentially amount to bribery to get the economically challenged into uniform.

For example, one "stop loss" incentive includes paying for the education and health care of the soldier and their children. This includes the unborn future children of the soldier. Taxpayers will pay for the health costs and education of the "stop loss" children decades into the future. Surely, the United States must live up to its promises to pay the benefits, but the nation's accountants cannot ignore these financial obligations while trying to balance the budget. These "stop loss" liabilities are unfunded and uncalculated obligations that America must recognize. If the nation wishes to treat its veterans fairly and have a balanced budget, anyway.

The United States is wasting so much money on foreign

occupations that rival nations have begun to comment. Some Chinese business leaders and diplomats have pointed critically to America's penchant for military adventure. Defending the huge trade deficits between the countries, the Chinese argue that American businesses have failed to invest profits back into their own enterprises. Additionally, they criticize American corporations for preferring the easy profits of war to the difficulties of remaining competitive in the corporate business world.

The Chinese case for squandered resources by America is a strong one, especially since none of the Pentagon budget is seeing true civilian accounting oversight. While the politicians in Washington, DC have argued about spending fractions of these war costs on domestic infrastructure or social programs, hundreds of billions annually evaporate in military actions across the globe with almost no debate. Even when there is a debate about a military action, there are no consequences for wild claims that in retrospect appear to be outright lies used to get support for the action. The last decades offer several examples of conscious manipulations of American foreign policy.

For example in the 1991 Gulf War, Americans were treated to tearful testimony in Congress from a Kuwaiti princess that Iraqi soldiers had broken into hospitals and thrown babies from incubators. As a princess of the Kuwaiti monarchy, she was believed without question. Of course, this alleged heinous act by Iraqi soldiers helped inflame passions in the US. This testimony was an out and out fiction, yet there were no consequences for any involved once it was exposed.

Afghanistan has long been nicknamed the graveyard of empires. Given the Soviet experience in the eighties, no one would ever have dreamed that the United States would even consider an invasion and occupation. To attack an entire nation for the acts of private individuals operating outside the bounds of national sovereignty seems cruel, especially in light of the historical suffering of the Afghan people. Unfortunately, there was a blood lust in the air. Americans were demanding that the 9/11 attacks be avenged.

Americans fooled themselves into believing that they were liberators of the Afghan people from the tyranny of the Taliban, but no

Afghan would see themselves as liberated today. That foolishness and cruelty were made clear when the final solution for bin Laden involved a small strike team over a decade later. Tens of thousands of boots on the ground had accomplished nothing and at the time of this writing the US and allies control barely half of Afghanistan after more than sixteen years of conflict.

Additionally, while the United States was engaged in Afghanistan, the United States citizenry was sold more fiction about Iraq. Americans were told the invasion and occupation of Iraq was necessary to prevent Iraq from using weapons of mass destruction. They were also told the invasion would cost less than one hundred billion dollars. On top of that grand fiction was added the extra plot twist that the Iraqis themselves would fund their own liberation. Through their frozen assets, Americans were assured, Iraqis would fund America's military assistance.

Though it made economic sense for the military-industrial complex, this military deployment into Iraq made no strategic sense. The United States had already subjugated Iraq in the twentieth century. The Kurds operated in an autonomous region, protected by the northern no-fly zone. In the South, the Shiites were similarly protected by a no-fly zone. Saddam Hussein was effectively defanged. In addition, Saddam Hussein was a westernized Muslim, in direct opposition to Al-Qaeda's fundamentalist Muslim philosophy.

Of course, Hussein was still making money off oil and perpetrating acts of terror on the ground within his own borders, but his ability to project his power was non-existent. Additionally, Al-Qaeda was a fundamentalist Islamic organization, and Iraq was led by a tie-wearing secular Muslim in Hussein. Given the rivalry between these two Muslim philosophies, almost all experts on the matter concluded that there was zero chance that Iraq and Al-Qaeda had joined forces or that they would do so in the future. Nonetheless, America invaded Iraq over the objections of most of the world. The chaos created has made the situation far worse in Middle East.

America has expended more than a trillion dollars in Iraq without a victory in that theater. Despite the alleged end of hostilities in Iraq, there are thousands of boots on the ground in old Babylon. It is understood, but cannot be overemphasized, that Iraq is still costing more than $100 billion annually for those boots on the ground. Again, there appear to be no consequences for military leaders given these negative outcomes.

The lack of victory on any front would seem to indicate incredible incompetence or a purposeful desire by some for the military actions to continue. Unfortunately, few in government even question this lack of progress. Instead, expansion of the global conflict into Syria is given serious consideration as is a strike against Iran. Military action can be very useful to politicians who wish to wrap themselves in the flag and very difficult to oppose for those trying to hold the military accountable. Such questions are easy to shout down with accusations of unpatriotic behavior and lack of support for the troops.

If no one can find the backbone to question the generals as to why there is no victory, the answer will never come. America has now fought for thrice the length of World War II and yet seems to have accomplished almost nothing. Unless one counts the lining of the pockets of wartime profiteers and emptying the national treasury as accomplishments.

Given the enormous technological advantages that the United States has enjoyed, it should be embarrassing to the generals that they have not won. Not only should these actions have been won, but won decisively in a timely fashion given these enormous advantages. If America's generals are embarrassed, they do not seem to show it. Somebody should remind them that World War II was only four years long against a technologically equal enemy. Today, the United States is unable to defeat enemies using homemade devices in some cases. Eisenhower would have fired these boys long ago!

However, rather than being fired, the generals are given more troops and money for an increasing number of military actions in the name of a global War on Terror. Yet there is no progress on any of the global fronts. America's coffers are empty, but the deployments continue. These undeclared wars have buoyed the stock prices of the military-industrial complex, but have done little to move forward any coherent American agenda or goals. The wars have been fought with little budgetary oversight and essentially been financed by Chinese bond purchases. Any confrontations with China from now until the nation repays this Chinese debt will always be colored by America's new status as a beggar nation.

The military-industrial complex is not a patriotic group. They are a for profit group with an eye to their bottom line. The fact that the money driving profits for the military-industrial complex is coming from Beijing does not cost their accountants any sleep. Americans must accept that the invasion of these nations by the United States may have been for the wrong reasons. These mistakes have played right into the hands of the Chinese government. Whether this consequence is through conscious or unconscious manipulations of military policy, the result is this nation's ability to stand against a Chinese deployment in Asia is crippled. The United States will have to consider scaling back military commitments to control its debt.

As long as the United States is pinned down in foreign occupations, it is vulnerable to military incursions against its true interests, domestically and worldwide. Even if the nation were able to unwind all the foreign occupations to discourage such incursions, neither the Chinese nor the Russians really fear the United States any longer. Though it may still be true neither nation can stand toe to toe with America in any given conflict, it is now clear that America does not have the financial wherewithal to sustain any long confrontation or deployment against a first rate adversary.

Iraq and Afghanistan have sapped military and financial resources, while boosting the profits of the military-industrial complex. Significant escalation anywhere else will stretch the military and tax the nation's financial resources further. Patriots of all stripes must accept the futility of these military actions across the globe. Real patriots will understand the United States can no longer sustain these military deployments without threatening the financial health of the United States.

The damage to the nation's bank account is not small, but the damage to America's reputation and honor has been catastrophic. America has suffered the tragic loss of the moral leadership bestowed upon it after World War II. This demotion is directly related to America's endless global military adventures. Americans continue to see the world through a WWII time lens, but that world is long gone.

America's Dangerous World War II Mythology

The world acknowledges that America never stood taller than in World War II. However, World War II was actually the second chapter of the Great War (WWI). It reflects a unique moment in world history. It is a moment in history that is essentially "sequel" to a precursor event. Americans do not usually see the two wars as connected the way the rest of the world does, because other than Pearl Harbor there was very little action on American soil. World War II has colored American ideas about war, as it should. Unfortunately, Americans only seem to recall the glory and little of the grit that was essential to that story.

Drawing conclusions about war, especially the economics of war, based upon the sequel, which World War II was, without recognizing the prequel, World War I, leads to many misconceptions. This American disconnect with the Great War has led to some very real misconceptions about war. These misconceptions make it easier to goad the American public to military action. American conclusions about WWII are flawed by a lack of historical perspective.

Some powerful myths about war have grown in American culture due to the uniqueness of the WWII experience in the United States. These myths are so powerful that many Americans accept them as proven facts. These ideas borne out of World War II have been leveraged to create further dogma. The military-industrial complex has annexed this mythology for its own ends and uses it for self-promotion.

Myth #1 - War Is Good For the Economy

Many Americans believe that war is good for the economy because the Depression appeared to be ended by WWII. However, FDR's New Deal had brought much relief to the nation by 1936–7. Unfortunately, worries about socialism in Congress and the financial classes curtailed New Deal programs, causing another downturn in the later years of the decade. The myth of war's economic benefits was strengthened by the fact that every one of the developed nations of the mid-twentieth century had their industrial infrastructure destroyed by war. Great Britain, Germany, Japan, China, and Russia/Soviet Union all had huge internal reconstruction to perform after the Second World War.

This reconstruction was made doubly difficult as it followed on top of the struggle to recover from the Great War. Two very destructive wars fought over two generations on their territories crippled Europe and Asia. An American economic hegemony was assured by 1945. Every potential competitor for the title of global economic leader was broken by the dual catastrophes of World War I and II.

America then used its immense economic output to make sure that there would be future markets for American goods via the Marshall Plan in Europe. General Douglas MacArthur's rebuilding in Japan followed a similar plan. To guarantee the markets would be there for American business, the United States made the markets in its own image. America has reaped the rewards for more than half a century of this strategic rebuilding of its former enemies immediately following WWII. However, that unique situation cannot be used to drive future economic decisions.

The fact that Nazi Germany rebuilt its manufacturing infrastructure, so quickly under Hitler also feeds this myth that war is good for a nation's economy. For some reason, it is often overlooked that rebuilding an economy is much easier when a nation does not pay workers a living wage or in the case of prison slave labor, pay the workers at all. Huge profits can be made at the expense of the dignity and freedom of the individual as was done by Hitler in Nazi Germany.

Americans easily forget that economies operating on a wartime footing tend to be tied more closely to the state with no need to provide workers a living wage. This industrial-military connection creates an authoritarian capitalism that can boost economic output quickly. Businesses love the guaranteed revenues and healthy profit margins from military customers. To some, the rightful name of the aforementioned political system is fascism.

Libertarian-Socialists do not dispute that wars can be good for economies, especially if the aggressor nation loots and pillages everything it can from the nations it conquers. Germany tried to do that at the beginning of World War II. The Nazis could not hold what they had gained due to the Allied choice to turn back Germany while fighting a holding action against Japan. A strategy meant to prevent Hitler from consolidating the natural resource gains he had made in the Middle East oil fields.

Looked at with ruthless eyes, the most abject failure of the neo-conservative toppling of Saddam Hussein through invasion and occupation is that it did not deliver the promised economic benefits. Control of the Iraq oil fields should have brought some very cheap gasoline among other financial benefits to the United States, but the exact opposite occurred. Whether this failure was due to: incompetence, corruption or ideological flaws will be debated for decades.

Libertarian-Socialists recognize that failure is real when one does the ruthless accounting of war and empire building. Libertarian-Socialists also recognize that during such confiscatory war, it can be difficult for the aggressor nation to invest in its own infrastructure, as it has to spend so much time occupying, administrating, exploiting and holding the vanquished. This was a different lesson from WWII that the Germans and Japanese understand far better than Americans.

The occupying nation must always expend resources to hold the occupied territories. In addition, depending upon the persistence and resistance of the occupied, it can be a net negative even when a nation is confiscating all that is valuable from the conquered. The people of Afghanistan, who sit upon a treasure trove of natural resources at a geopolitical crossroads, have made it a habit of reminding empires through the centuries of the costs to hold and occupy the unwilling.

Myth #2 - World War II Made America the World's Police

Another myth from WWII is that all subsequent military engagements are NOT war, but police actions and therefore no formal declaration of war need be declared. Since World War II America has spent trillions of dollars on the Korean War, the Vietnam War, the Gulf War, et al and none of these wars have been declared. The patriotic libertarian and the patriotic socialist easily agree that the executive branch of government must have some latitude to deploy troops for quick response in this dangerous world. Nonetheless, the legislative branch is where wars should be given the official backing of the people. The patriotic libertarian and the patriotic socialist are in complete agreement; the aforementioned "police actions" were in fact wars, since no one refers to the Indo-China conflict as the Vietnam Police Action. Certainly not those that fought in that engagement.

Short-term troop deployments are one thing, but multi-year foreign occupations and invasions must be supported by a declaration of war. A full debate of the American Congress puts issues of killing and the making of war more clearly in front of the politicians. Pangs of conscience are possible even in this jaded crowd of sociopaths. The military-industrial complex understands a formal declaration of war can be very difficult to achieve without an EMINENT threat. Eminent threats are actually rare, so better to have these slowly growing conflicts that eventually become full blown long-term wars without having to face the public debate in the beginning. The profits still roll in, just slower at first.

The legislative branch has shown itself to be somewhat spineless on the issue of war declarations and has repeatedly allowed executive branch troop deployments to drag on without any oversight, let alone a formal declaration of war. Legislative cowardice allowed Korea, Vietnam, Desert Storm, Afghanistan and Iraq to be prosecuted with no formal declaration of war. Though in the case of Korea, President Harry Truman's coining of the term "police action" did put the legislative branch back on its heels.

In the case of the latter three, the legislative branch passed Authorizations to Use Military Force instead of debating a formal declaration of war. A formal declaration of war gives the executive branch additional powers. In the case of war, libertarian-socialists understand a need for the commander-in-chief to have more power, and demoting the Congress once war is actually declared. This Constitutional paradox makes the formal debate of a declaration of war so important. If soldiers are to die, then the Congress must believe so strongly that war is necessary that it essentially cedes some of its powers for the duration. Instead, the legislative branch has sent soldiers into harm's way without an honest debate about WAR. Congress preserves its power and abrogates itself of constitutional obligations through the authorization to use military force also known as an AUMF.

This is where citizens must demand a formal declaration of war every time troops are deployed for extended periods. This prevents the legislature from turning its back on wartime responsibilities to publicly debate the goals for military action and then step back and let the commander-in-chief prosecute the war. Congress has proven they lack the political will without pressure from the people to debate a formal declaration of war no matter the consequences of their avoidance. Despite the many thousands of casualties in Korea, Vietnam, Afghanistan, and Iraq since World War II, Congress has not debated a war declaration resolution in 75 years!

Myth #3 - The American Military Has Superpowers

One reason that the public allows these AUMFs is that mythology of WWII. The American military is believed to have super powers that can solve all manner of problems across the planet, at least if those powers are brought to bear forcefully. This belief is an article of faith. It is held with an almost religious fervor. This is not hyperbole as those that lived through it saw the defeat of the Third Reich as vanquishing Satan. Unfortunately, the Greatest Generation is no more and the circumstances of their victory a unique moment in time. The special powers fueled by unlimited money and an unsurpassed economic power are nearly exhausted. The world has changed too much. The United States can only work on itself and cannot control global evolution.

The actions of this century ended America's status as the sole superpower. Though the libertarian-socialist agenda can help return America to greatness, the nation is not likely to regain sole superpower status. This truth must be accepted for the nation to evolve. America may be able to hold a position as a first among equals and stabilize finances, but it will be difficult to regain the historic super powers that most Americans have believed in for so long.

From the world's point of view, if the United States were still a superpower, it would have successfully prosecuted the wars in Afghanistan and Iraq. WWII was fought against a technologically equal military force and in some cases, a technological edge was held by the Axis powers. However, Hitler and Tojo were defeated in four years. The United States has been in Afghanistan for over 16 years, while being in and out of the Middle East Theater for even longer than that. What does victory look like against this technologically inferior opponent and why cannot America achieve it?

The close alliance between the nation's politicians with the military-industrial complex allows wartime profiteers silently to steer American foreign policy in directions that are not in the best interest of this nation. The most important consequence of this hijacking of the United States military by private corporate interests is that Americans must accept the fact the nation will no longer be able to draw upon its historic military super powers. In the nineties, America was perceived as the lone superpower. The world appeared to be in the beginnings of a Pax Americana. For the first time in many, many years, it was possible to travel to almost any place on the planet and not be in fear of conflict at the turn of the twenty-first century. Unfortunately, that all began to unravel with the 9/11 attacks and then the world was torn apart by the preemptive strike on Baghdad shattering the superpower mythology of the USA as the world's police force.

The United States must get used to being a nation that has peers. The patriotic libertarian and the patriotic socialist reluctantly agree and acknowledge that saber rattling has little effect on America's most formidable enemies now. The United States now exists in a dangerous multi-polar world, which has yet to solidify into stable power blocs.

America must recognize that it no longer resides in the bi-polar world of the Cold War or the unilateral Pax Americana that existed after the fall of the Soviet Union. The globe has in fact returned to the extremely dangerous and complicated multi-polar world that preceded the First Great World War. The world recognizes the return to a multi-polar state of affairs, but Americans are blinded by their myths and do not see the danger.

Myth #4 - War Drives Invention and Innovation

One of the most enduring myths of World War II is that war drives invention and innovation. This is considered an unassailable fact in some quarters. The debate between the patriotic libertarian and the patriotic socialist brought this myth under close inspection and it does not stand up. History does not support this contention of great technological advance only occurs through war. War and the pressure to weaponize all technology often enhances great inventions, there is no question, but there is more nuance to be examined.

Libertarian-Socialists need to remind Americans of the surprising number of the great inventions that have changed the world over the last couple of centuries that were NOT created by or for war. The list of the great peacetime inventions is actually quite long: the bicycle, automobile, telephone, radio, television, electric light, airplane, steam ships and locomotives are peacetime inventions all. These are undeniable peacetime inventions. Inventions created because of the peacetime information sharing that promotes huge leaps in creativity.

Some inventions seem to be undeniably weapons of war, but were peacetime ideas. The rocket was "reinvented" by American Robert Goddard after the ancient Chinese technology had been lost centuries before. The computer came about in the thirties before World War II, though code breaking drove an incredible advancement of it during that war. Even the basic ideas of how to use nuclear fission to create energy were there before WWII drove the United States to weaponize it as the first atomic bomb. There is no denying that war can drive the refinement of existing technologies to more power and efficiency. However, history indicates that seminal technological leaps come from the synergies created through peace, not war.

There is a simple reason for the creativity found in peacetime and lack of it during wartime and that is the ever-present specter of national security interests. Wartime tends to lock up knowledge, not distribute it freely. Secrecy causes a loss of innovation. Americans might want to consider the history of its greatest rival, China, for confirmation. A thousand years ago, China was a country with huge technological leads on the rest of the world. This lead included gunpowder, rockets, and bombs which were in the Chinese arsenal centuries before they appeared in the West. Somehow, though, this technological lead had disappeared by the time of the Opium Wars in the 19th century. The mainstream history of China that Westerners traditionally heard indicated these technological advantages were never weaponized, but that is myth.

The world is now facing recent revelations in Chinese archaeology and history that indicate these technologies were weaponized. The Chinese did not just build fireworks; they built bombs and other explosive missiles. The Chinese enjoyed a technological advantage militarily. They deployed these weapons against their enemies controlling an enormous portion of the Asian continent. With such a technological lead, how did the Chinese fall so far behind? These weapons existed at the time of Marco Polo, but these were likely hidden from a foreigner. Despite the national security interests of China, the secrets of gunpowder eventually did make it to Europe. Europe was a chaotic geopolitical battleground and ideas on how to weaponize gunpowder spread quickly and widely. The lack of effective secrecy along with nationalist conflicts on the European continent allowed for far more rapid development of gunpowder weaponry.

The Chinese held a technological lead, but it began to shrink. The Chinese became more insular and inward looking. As their military advantage shrank, the Chinese attempted to further lock down the secrets of this technological lead. Gunpowder became a national security secret to preserve a military advantage. Unfortunately, over time this secrecy eroded the Chinese technological lead. As China sought to cut-off contact with the outside world, they were cutting off the free exchange of ideas, which led to the loss of their technological advantage.

Since WWII, the US government has largely controlled innovation, creating a very similar dynamic. It is harder to find late twentieth century examples of peacetime inventions, because true peacetime has not existed since the Cold War. One world changing invention that has come is the Internet, which started out as a DARPA military project. The internet has become a source of further great innovation, in spite of the government and military's desires to keep the secrets locked away. However, even this is based upon a peacetime invention...the computer.

The internet was invented in the sixties and enhanced in the relative peacetime of the seventies. Invented in this special time in America, it is a special case. Even under military oversight, it is an innovative exception due to the rebellious spirit of the time in the United States. It was this rebellious attitude that was driving innovation despite military desires for secrecy. Additionally, what the world sees as the internet is actually the World Wide Web. The "www" that precedes so many websites stands for the World Wide Web and a foreigner, Tim Berners-Lee, invented this. The internet blossomed as a public entity, because the inventors refused to cooperate with the military-industrial complex thus allowing anyone, even non-Americans, to innovate on the platform.

Such rebellion could not occur today, because the freedom of the individual has been greatly curtailed (another reason to protect privacy) in the United States since the mid-20th century. Here we have an example of a military invention whose great contributions to the peacetime infrastructure were forced upon it by the rebellious inventors of the technology. The inventors refused to make its architecture secret or embed surveillance technologies within it, allowing a foreigner like Berners-Lee to build the World Wide Web. Without these rebels, the original hackers forcing an open and transparent design, the internet never could have become the great global information highway.

Myth #5 - Secrecy Preserves Technological Advantage

This may be the toughest myth to disprove. It does seem to go against common sense when one does not think deeply about it. Of course, if one has a serious technological advantage, it is hard to share when one is only thinking from the point of view of the military. In the short term, the technological military advantage is preserved, but over the long haul it causes the advantage to be eroded.

The military secrecy does not just extend to foreign actors. The secrecy becomes very tight domestically as well to prevent civilians from leaking the information. This means cutting edge technology is only in the hands of the military which tends to have a very narrow view of how technology will be developed and advanced. Over time, domestic civilian research and development is stunted. The great leap forward into some new technological paradigm that will always come occurs elsewhere.

Secrecy limits the sharing of information, and without a collaborative knowledgebase, the synergies that accelerate development and invention simply cannot happen. In the case of China, it took hundreds of years before the European innovation machine surpassed the Chinese. It took time, but the West did indeed eclipse Chinese technological advantages by the late 18th century and early 19th century. When the two sides met again, China was at a distinct disadvantage.

Currently, the pace of change is far greater. Presuming the United States still has an advantage; it is evaporating at quite a rate. Libertarian-Socialists must spread the word that the American advantage is tenuous. The Chinese are on the moon, making real advances in quantum computing and may have already eclipsed the US in the communication space. Patriots must spur citizens to regain the transparency peacetime brings to jump start real innovation in America again. It will be a tragic irony for the West, if we meet the East again in conflict this century with the exact opposite outcome.

Unwinding Jobs Tied To the Defense Department

Despite clear evidence that America's global military deployments are sapping the nation's resources, unwinding the massive investment in war machinery will not be easy. Unfortunately, military deployments are good for many businesses that make profits off weapons and logistics. Those businesses now dominate the American business landscape.

Not to spend on these deployments risks jobs for sure. This is not a common talking point in support of these military actions, but the job connection is implicitly understood. The patriotic libertarian and the patriotic socialist agree that jobs for war is not an ethical position. Nonetheless, jobs are at great risk were there a curtailment of America's foreign entanglements. Libertarian-Socialists must understand this truth, if they are to reach their fellow Americans and change minds.

Many Americans are employed directly or tangentially in the defense industry. Sadly, the loss of one's job is far more important to most Americans than the cost of any civilian casualty in a far-off war. A war they are told is necessary. On the surface, the debate will always appear to be about national security, but unconsciously too many Americans know their job requires the building of more war birds, air craft carriers etc.

It is on the financial front that curtailing the conflict economy will happen, voluntarily or involuntarily. History is littered with nations and empires that sapped their strength and emptied their treasuries through constant conflict. As much as humanitarians believe the answer to ending America's global military deployment is to worry the American conscience, it is more likely that the balance sheet will finally get the attention of American citizens.

The military-industrial complex will keep pushing for more conflict no matter how bad it is for the overall economy in the long-term. Since corporations are not patriotic, they will continue to siphon resources from the United States until there are no more resources. At which point the multi-national corporation will simply look for new customers elsewhere. They will not shed a tear about the damage to America's economy or balance sheet.

American citizens will care and there is still time to convince them that infrastructure investments are the best way to spend America's dwindling dollars. The United States currently makes few investments in its own infrastructure or in its own people. This is due to budget constraints caused by the costs of the foreign wars.

Time is no longer on America's side. It is the twenty-first century. The nation has been neglecting its infrastructure for too long. Across America, bridges are nearing collapse, the social safety net is being shredded and the education of children has become third-rate. At the same time, the United States has been on a wartime footing for almost the entire twenty-first century.

Selling the infrastructure investment over the patriotic puffery of military deployments is difficult. Selling the slower gradual growth brought about by investment in infrastructure will not be easy. Economists agree, war can create short-term economic activity, but it creates no lasting infrastructure or other capitalized investment that will payoff far in the future. Infrastructure investment is very expensive and does not necessarily give the same amount of short-term economic benefit that the defense industry can supply. There are enormous long-term benefits, economic and otherwise from infrastructure investment, but they require patience to come to fruition. Patience is a commodity that requires some faith and belief. These need the support of a clear patriotic libertarian-socialist vision.

The patriotic libertarian and the patriotic socialist agree that the time is overdue to refresh the infrastructure for continued economic growth. These infrastructure projects can produce enormous future boosts to the economy providing uncounted jobs. Two perfect examples of how a huge infrastructure investment can pay dividends are the Republican Eisenhower's superhighway program and rural electrification under the Democrat, FDR.

In both these cases, the investments were so enormous that they were measured in percentage of GDP. However, the GDP growth that followed in the long term has paid off many times over. The payoffs of infrastructure investment cannot be calculated with any exactitude due to the difficulties of predicting the events of future decades. However, the benefits are real despite being hard to visualize completely.

The reinvestment cannot happen with the current budgetary constraints that the global War on Terror puts on the nation. America cannot build out its infrastructure to gain these future synergies as long as it is mired in military conflicts around the globe. The difficult process of scaling back the American military presence across the planet is a necessity for the United States to invest in itself.

That difficult process will involve retooling and retraining broadly due to the large amount of weapon manufacture that is part of American economic activity. Many politicians and business leaders will balk at this retooling as it will require investments in machinery not tailored to military conflict. The mythology of World War II will be leveraged to prevent this scaling back of the defense industry.

Libertarian-Socialists should expect that the dangers of appeasement will be trotted out in all their forms to keep the military deployments going. However, libertarian-socialists will warn against the dangerous groupthink of fighting the last war. One can expect that the quotes from British Prime Minister Neville Chamberlain to be a part of the conversation and these should be met with reminders of how the Nazis outflanked the Maginot Line created by French generals fighting the "last war". The last war at that time was the First World War and the Maginot Line failed to take into account technological advancement.

Driven by patriotism, thinking Americans are compelled to question the huge military commitment the United States has taken on. When the number of Americans dying at the hand of other Americans is increasing, foreign deployments make less sense. Indeed, as the war with non-state adversaries has gone on four times as long WWII, surely Americans will see the folly of it.

Nonetheless, patriots care about their fellow Americans and understand that many individuals will lose their jobs were the military commitments and weapons programs ended in a short time. There is also the understanding that this quick end could be brought on involuntarily by a sudden lack of money. It is this understanding that brings about the urgency in patriots to change the country's wartime footing.

The patriotic libertarian and the patriotic socialist can agree on the need for scaling back the military commitments of the United States. Yet, so many jobs are based upon Department of Defense contracts that an immediate change of direction will cause hardship all across the economy. An unwinding of American military commitments is very complex. How can this scaling back be done without causing a massive loss of jobs within the economy? This question needs an answer for Americans to support a roll back.

The American space program has been pared down to the bare bones and is a mere shadow of its former self. The program that put the first human on another planet is starved for funding. With all America's budgetary problems, it is easy to cut the space program. The dividends from investing in space technologies are highly speculative and hard to predict. Those technological leaps that pursuing a space program provides have national security implications, though. Economic efficiencies can come from space-related inventions. Often space technologies can be rather easily weaponized as well, if the need arises.

In this context, libertarian-socialists must convince America that it should not cede a moon base to China! Frozen water has been verified in moon craters in very large quantities. Quantities that provide a moon base with all the raw materials for maintaining an independent existence. Water has its obvious uses, but it can also be split at the molecular level to provide fuel, hydrogen, and atmosphere, oxygen, for the base. A base could be engaged in mining operations, most likely, but many other high tech projects as well.

With so much of America's military budget geared to supply large foreign occupations, the United States lacks the innovations that would occur in the healthy research and development budget of a rich nation. America lacks the funding to push research and development projects, like the United States space program of the sixties. Ending foreign occupation could immediately fund a new push to colonize beyond Earth.

This funding should be directly pressed into re-energizing the American space program. Without a quick pivot of the funding into a similar enterprise, like a space program, the unemployed defense workers become harder to employ. This would not simply be a useless hiring program either. The United States should regain its leadership in space, because it can spark innovation as well as employ citizens. Patriotic libertarian-socialists can spark enthusiasm when such a win-win scenario is explained.

America's space program is so starved for funding that it leans heavily upon the Russian capabilities to get things done. This is one reason why being an astronaut in the United States requires one to be able to speak Russian. In the new multi-polar world, the United States cannot afford to have the Chinese and Russian space programs expanding, while America retires the shuttles. Asking the private sector to pick up the slack is an insufficient response.

A renewed Space Race will create jobs that are at least similar to many of the defense industry jobs that will be lost in the Great Unwinding of America's global military deployments. Not to mention, there are actually some clear military advantages to investing in our space program. Doubters need only read Robert Heinlein's The Moon is a Harsh Mistress. In that novel, the military benefits of the "high ground" continue despite technological change.

Identity in America

Identity politics are destroying the nation. This book must step on the third rail of American politics. Even though the central premise of this book is that America has good reason for hope, race and gender relations represent a reason for pessimism. The libertarian-socialist plan is real and viable. It will succeed if implemented, but the division fueled by identity politics can derail it all. In America, to discuss race with any honesty is to enter a dangerous minefield. It is such a volatile issue that people have learned not to speak openly about exactly what they feel.

The post-racial society that was the dream, no longer seems possible in the current climate. Can America evolve into a nation that owns its past and forgives itself? A failure to do so will very likely lead to the United States ceasing to be a nation. Forgiveness is key. The patriotic libertarian and the patriotic socialist are able to come to agreements, because they believe that each is a patriotic American. There is no need to hyphenate anything in that appellation.

This is the greatest single hurdle facing the United States. There are many obstacles to the continuation of the republic, but this one seems the most pernicious and intractable. It is libertarian-socialism's central tenet that tolerance is the solution to the enduring pain of the racial tension in America. This tension represents a primary obstacle to tolerance. This book is a practical and pragmatic plan that can return America to greatness and restore the republic.

The patriotic libertarian and the patriotic socialist believe in a color-blind country of ideas, energy, industry, freedom and justice for ALL regardless of their gender, race or religion. They believe it is possible for the pie to be made larger, if the proper policies are implemented.

What will you do with this political agenda? Continue to fight old battles from the past? These are battles that are financed by moneyed power to keep hundreds of millions of poor and middle class Americans fighting with each other instead of joining together.

These are ideas that can be implemented, if the people have the will and the tolerance. Do you?

Dedication

This book is dedicated to my loyal companion, Laker, who near the end of her life regularly got me up at 4 AM to pursue this project to completion. I love you Doggie Girl. Thank you, Lakey.